BEETHOVEN'S
String Quartet in C-sharp Minor, Op. 131

BEETHOVEN'S
String Quartet in C-sharp Minor, Op. 131

NANCY NOVEMBER

OXFORD
UNIVERSITY PRESS

Oxford University Press is a department of the University of Oxford. It furthers the University's objective of excellence in research, scholarship, and education by publishing worldwide. Oxford is a registered trade mark of Oxford University Press in the UK and certain other countries.

Published in the United States of America by Oxford University Press
198 Madison Avenue, New York, NY 10016, United States of America.

© Oxford University Press 2021

Library of Congress Cataloging-in-Publication Data
Names: November, Nancy, author.
Title: Beethoven's String quartet in C-sharp minor, op. 131 / Nancy November.
Description: New York : Oxford University Press, 2021. | Series: Oxford keynotes series | Includes bibliographical references and index.
Identifiers: LCCN 2020055035 (print) | LCCN 2020055036 (ebook) | ISBN 9780190059200 (hardback) | ISBN 9780190059217 (paperback) | ISBN 9780190059231 (epub) | ISBN 9780190059248 (online) ·
Subjects: LCSH: Beethoven, Ludwig van, 1770-1827. Quartets, violins (2), viola, cello, no. 14, op. 131, C# minor.
Classification: LCC ML410.B42 N79 2021 (print) | LCC ML410.B42 (ebook) | DDC 785/.7194092—dc23
LC record available at https://lccn.loc.gov/2020055035
LC ebook record available at https://lccn.loc.gov/2020055036

DOI: 10.1093/oso/9780190059200.001.0001

9 8 7 6 5 4 3 2 1
Paperback printed by Marquis, Canada
Hardback printed by Bridgeport National Bindery, Inc., United States of America

Oxford Keynotes reimagines the canons of Western music for the twenty-first century. With each of its volumes dedicated to a single composition or album, the series provides an informed, critical, and provocative companion to music as artwork and experience. Books in the series explore how works of music have engaged listeners, performers, artists, and others through history and in the present. They illuminate the roles of musicians and musics in shaping Western cultures and societies, and they seek to spark discussion of ongoing transitions in contemporary musical landscapes. Each approaches its key work in a unique way, tailored to the distinct opportunities that the work presents. Targeted at performers, curious listeners, and advanced undergraduates, volumes in the series are written by expert and engaging voices in their fields, and will therefore be of significant interest to scholars and critics as well.

In selecting titles for the series, Oxford Keynotes balances two ways of defining the canons of Western music: as lists of works that critics and scholars deem to have articulated key moments in the history of the art, and as lists of works that comprise the bulk of what consumers listen to, purchase, and perform today. Often, the two lists intersect, but the overlap is imperfect. While not neglecting the first, Oxford Keynotes gives considerable weight to the second. It confronts the musicological canon with the living repertoire of performance and recording in classical, popular, jazz, and other idioms. And it seeks to expand that living repertoire through the latest musicological research.

Kevin Bartig
Michigan State University

CONTENTS

ACKNOWLEDGMENTS

THIS BOOK WAS INSPIRED by a lecture given on the subject, which provoked an unusual degree of attentive listening, followed by lively discussion. Kevin Karnes then provided useful feedback and enthusiastically encouraged the development of this material into a book, the research for which was enabled by generous support from the University of Auckland during my 2019 sabbatical leave. I am indebted to Christine Siegert, Director of Beethoven-Haus Archive and Publishing for her collegiality and continued support of my research, and to the librarians at Beethoven-Haus, in particular Stephanie Kuban and Dorothea Geffert. I am indebted to Janet Hughes and Janet November for assistance with editorial suggestions and proofreading; to Sam Girling for setting the musical examples.

This book is dedicated to my son Nikolaus, who, like Op. 131, is always overflowing with new and unusual ideas.

INTRODUCTION

IN THE LIVES OF great artists, the late or last works are often considered to be the greatest, the flowering or crowning of all that came before. This phenomenon, the valuing of "late" creations, artistic creations in particular, is perhaps nowhere more obvious than in connection with Beethoven. The late works, especially the late quartets, late piano sonatas, and the last symphony (the Ninth), are much discussed, much performed, and highly prized. In the case of Beethoven's String Quartet in C-sharp minor, Op. 131 (1826), this canonization is everywhere apparent. The work is not only firmly a part of the scholarly canon, the performing canon, and the pedagogical canon, but also makes its presence felt in popular culture, notably in film (for example, *A Late Quartet*, 2012). Yet in recent times, the

Beethoven's String Quartet in C-sharp Minor, Op. 131. Nancy November, Oxford University Press.
© Oxford University Press 2021. DOI: 10.1093/oso/9780190059200.003.0001

terms in which the C-sharp minor quartet is discussed and presented tend to undermine the work's power. Although it is held up as a masterpiece, Op. 131 has often been understood in monochrome terms, as a work portraying tragedy, struggle, loss, and lack.

This book takes the modern-day listener well beyond these categories of adversity or deficit. It goes back to early reception documents, including Beethoven's own writings about the work, to help the listener reinterpret the work and re-hear it. Analyses are multivalent, taking into account aspects of physicality as well as the sonic; these are geared toward allowing the reader to access earlier modes of listening and interpretation, those of listeners who celebrated the work precisely for its plenitude, its richness of invention or fantasy (in Beethoven's own words). As connoisseur listeners of Beethoven's day implied, Op. 131 is filled with diverse musical ideas (just like a fantasia), and with a new kind of string quartet writing that is calculated to promote sustained, engaged listening. Placing this work in the context of an emerging ideology of silent or "serious" listening in Beethoven's Europe, I consider how this particular "late" quartet could speak with special eloquence to a highly select but passionately enthusiastic audience. I also examine how and why the reception of Op. 131 has changed so profoundly from Beethoven's time to our own.

The book emphasizes reception history, with a particular focus on how various listeners have heard the work, historically and today. My multi-faceted approach is new: I study a variety of relevant sources in order to obtain a well-rounded understanding of reception that takes account not only of mainstream scholarship, but also more popular media such as film and television. I explore historical listening in connection with Op. 131 through reviews, images, eyewitness accounts, and my analyses of the music itself. Popular media, and other musical compositions and arrangements, are included here as reception documents that speak to how listeners have re-heard the work and made it intelligible in their own terms and according to their aesthetic priorities, over nearly two hundred years.

CHAPTER 1

RE-HEARING OP. 131

[Op. 131 is] patched together from pieces filched here and there.
—Beethoven to Schott, August 1826.[1]

BEETHOVEN'S FIVE "LATE" QUARTETS have always provoked fierce reactions and strong opinions. Critics and scholars have taken extreme positions on them and disagreed often, but over time a thread of shifting orthodoxy can be traced through the history of writings about these works. Wagner's essay *Beethoven* (1870) has been credited with bringing about one huge and crucial shift, turning around the reception of the late quartets completely: before Wagner, they were widely perceived as chaotic works from a deaf madman; after Wagner, they came to be seen

Beethoven's String Quartet in C-sharp Minor, Op. 131. Nancy November, Oxford University Press.

as transcendent, the finest works of a genius.[2] In particular, as K. M. Knittel shows, Wagner offered a new take on disability and creativity. Wagner interprets deafness as a powerful enabling force that allows Beethoven to retreat within himself to truly *listen*. So, far from disabling him as a composer, his loss of hearing frees him to realize his highest artistic ideals, for which the String Quartet in C-sharp minor, Op. 131, represents the paradigm.[3]

The reception of the late string quartets generally follows from this reevaluation—although we could debate the strong emphasis on Wagner as turning point. But with Op. 131 the story is more complicated, and at times it runs counter to the post-Wagner narrative. Yes, with rare exceptions, the work has been held up since the late nineteenth century as the greatest of the five. But the basis of the greatness is far from agreed. The most common observation about the character of Op. 131 is that the work is full of divergent ideas, sharp contrasts, and fantasy that seems to be spontaneous. Gustav Nottebohm observed in 1887 that the work gives an overriding "impression of an improvisation" ("Eindruck einer Improvisation"),[4] and this idea echoes through many later writings about the work. It seems to encourage authors to demonstrate elaborately and repeatedly that Op. 131 is coherent regardless: again and again they analyze the work in detail to reveal unity and underlying logic. It is almost as if modern-day scholars are responding to the work's "patchwork" character—as Beethoven himself described it, in jest with a grain of truth, in a letter to Schott of August 1826—and defending the composer and work against the charge that it demonstrates insufficient coherence.

So although Op. 131 has attracted the kind of praise we have come to expect since Wagner for a "late" Beethoven work, its reception on examination is mixed, and the post-Wagner shift starts to look less seismic. Clearly the five "late" quartets cannot always be taken as a group. The last of them, Op. 135 in F major, has long been thought retrogressive because it seems less radical than the other five late quartets.[5] For Op. 131, the opposite seems to be true: it is outwardly almost *too* radical, so its inward coherence has been actively construed by critics with an agenda of reclamation.

WAGNER, HELM, AND INWARD LISTENING

Wagner was the first to offer a reading of Op. 131 that tries to account comprehensively for its inner coherence. He focuses particularly on Op. 131 and the Ninth Symphony in the *Beethoven* essay because these revolutionary works had aroused his interest in Beethoven's late music, and stresses their functions of preaching and teaching:

> Their effect upon the hearer is that of setting him free from the sense of guilt, just as their after-effect is a feeling of "paradise lost". . . Thus these wonderful works preach repentance and atonement in the deepest sense of a divine revelation . . . the aesthetic idea of the *Sublime* is alone applicable here . . .[6]

The idea that the late works are somehow spiritually instructive or reforming recurs widely. But Wagner interprets this pedagogical function to serve his own nationalist agenda, rather than to illuminate Beethoven's work. Wagner constructs a German compositional lineage starting with J.

S. Bach, who becomes Beethoven's main guide, his music Beethoven's Bible.[7] Wagner was covertly defining his own German musical pedigree.

These religious metaphors serve to conflate Beethoven's biography and his work in the most compelling way for Christians of Wagner's day, to offer a programmatic means of understanding Op. 131's inner coherence. Op. 131 apparently reveals to us how Beethoven was divinely inspired: "If we wish to picture to ourselves a day in the life of our Saint, one of the master's own wonderful pieces may serve as a counterpoint. . . . I shall choose, then, to illustrate such a genuine 'Beethoven day' by the light of its inmost occurrences, his great string quartet in C-sharp minor."[8] Op. 131, then, gives us the most intimate glimpse of the private artist, charting his progression from "communing with God" to "glances to the outer world," then returning to his inner vision.

Wagner's picturing of Op. 131 as a "Beethoven [Saint/ Christ] day" resonated with the popular idea of Beethoven's divinity, which was also depicted by visual artists.[9] An example is August Borckmann's *Beethoven und das Razumovsky'sche Quartet* (1872), painted just a few years after Wagner penned the *Beethoven* essay (Figure 1.1). Beethoven, swathed in light, is the center of the composition and of rapt attention from musicians and audience; among them is Haydn, who might be understood as "the Father" (he was often referred to as "papa Haydn"), Beethoven as "the Son," and the performers and listeners as twelve devoted apostles.[10]

Wagner's *Beethoven* essay contributed to the philosophical groundwork for new claims about the late works' greatness not only in terms of their inner coherence, but with

FIGURE 1.1   August Borckmann, *Beethoven und das Rasumowsky'sche Quartett*. Photographic reproduction from 1880–90 of the original painting of 1872. 63.0 × 75.8 cm. Below the picture one reads the following names of the people depicted (from left to right): "C. Czerni [*sic*]. / Haydn. / Fürstin Lichnowsky. / Baronin Dorothea von Erdmannsdorf. / Beethoven. / Schuppanzigh. / Anton Kraft. / Albrechtsberger. / Sina. / Weiss." (Courtesy of Beethoven-Haus, Bonn.)

specific reference to Beethoven's deafness. Wagner's concern with listening is central. He draws on Schopenhauer's idea of the "inner eye": deafness lets Beethoven shut out the external world of appearances and objects to listen only with his "inner ear." Schopenhauer makes a distinction between the outward act of hearing and the inward act of *listening*. And Wagner draws a parallel between hearing versus listening on the one hand, and seeing versus perceiving, envisioning, and prophesying on the other. He likens "deep" listening to "the condition of somnambulistic clairvoyance," the only state in which "we immediately partake of the musician's world," and observes that listening confounds the processing of input from the other senses: "everyone can observe the effect of music to be such that, during its influence, our vision is enfeebled, until, though with our eyes open, we still do not see clearly."[11] To clinch the point, he likens Beethoven to Tiresias, the blind prophet of Greek mythology:

> A musician without hearing! Could a blind painter be imagined? But we know of a blind *Seer*. Tiresias, to whom the phenomenal world was closed, but who, with inward vision, saw the basis of all phenomena,—the deaf musician who listens to his inner harmonies undisturbed by the noise of life, who speaks from the depths to a world that has nothing more to say to him—now resembles the seer.[12]

The idea that the late works entail a special, deeply internalized, spiritual, non-visual listening is problematic; so is the assumption that Beethoven composed them in response to mainly internal drives and dictates. The modes of listening that Beethoven developed are not simply related to the deafness; not necessarily connected to eventual "greatness"; and probably not related at all to being "cut off" from external reality. Beethoven was far from unaware of contemporary listeners and the contexts in which they listened. What he could not hear directly he could perceive in other ways, by listeners' observation or using his conversation books, for example.[13] And when he could no longer hear, he could remember. Joseph Kerman hears Dorabella, from Mozart's *Così fan tutte*, in No. 2 from Op. 131: she may have been stored away in Beethoven's aural memory.[14] The idea is compelling: in 1820s Vienna Italian opera was at the height of popularity with theater-goers and in chamber music arrangements for the home.

Yet scholars since Wagner have built on the idea that these late quartets were essentially "cut off" from the external world, attributing some metaphysical and spiritual meanings, but concentrating more on the formal analysis of purely musical meanings. Most scholars who write about Op. 131 are still focused on the score in a way that makes listening—perceiving in ways that accrue and change during a performance—secondary. Listeners are mentioned from time to time, but are mostly assumed to be ideal, expert listeners.

This approach emerges with Theodor Helm's views in the late nineteenth century, taking firm hold in the twentieth century. Helm's writings on the Beethoven quartets started to appear three years after Wagner's *Beethoven* essay, and were arguably even more influential.[15] He praises the late quartets in fulsome terms and adopts Wagner's teleological narrative, giving it an analytical grounding. In the case of Op. 131 he adds analytical detail to Wagner's expressive sketch, with numerous musical examples. Like Wagner, Helm maintained that only in his complete deafness did Beethoven truly begin to "listen," in a sense that was necessarily inward. The late quartets are "stamped with Beethoven's innermost self-confession, without a backward glance on applause or displeasure of the public, written by the master for himself out of inner need."[16] He recognizes the great originality and variety in the late works, but stresses above all their unity, especially in the logic and interconnections of Op. 131:

> The most outstanding characteristic features of Beethoven's last compositions: . . . vivid clarity and strict logic, the meaningful enunciation of content, down to every single bar, every note, we find in the C-sharp minor quartet . . .[17]

Helm sets the tone for later writers on Op. 131 by demonstrating the work's unity. First of all, he explains the unity of Op. 131 in expressive terms (like Wagner and other music critics of the day), describing a narrative of victory of a kind we would now more readily connect with Beethoven's middle-period works, especially the Fifth Symphony.[18] The C-sharp minor quartet is

> The elevation of the noble man's soul from the darkest night of deepest melancholy to liberating humor, to the victorious fighting down of fate's hostile demons, to the inner reconciliation.[19]

But Helm also examines the work's inner coherence in extensive analytic detail. His discussion of Op. 131 is the longest of his analyses of Beethoven's quartets, suggesting a need for defense even though he finds "vivid clarity" and "strict logic" in the work. Helm's comments on the recurrence of the opening idea in No. 7 have been especially influential. The second main group of themes, he says,

> gives way to a deeply painful lament, the motive of which is strikingly reminiscent of that of the first movement of the C-sharp minor quartet (you only have to change the half notes, and you have exactly the first half of that fugato motive).[20]

FIGURE 1.2   Musical examples from Helm's *Beethoven's Streichquartette*, showing (i) the opening motive, and (ii) the second theme of the finale (pp. 232 and 262).

After Helm, scholars reinterpreted this recollection of the opening idea in the Finale explicitly in terms of unity—virtually everyone mentioned it, and Kerman dwelt on it at length. The resemblance to the opening figure is clear enough if one *visually* rearranges the four notes in question to resemble the opening motive. Helm's reader needed to flip back a mere twenty-eight pages to compare the musical example from the finale to "Motiv a" from No. 1 (see Figure 1.2). But in terms of aural memory he was demanding quite a cognitive stretch from listeners. This recall of the opening tetrachord is undeniably difficult to hear on first pass—it requires attentive long-range listening to more than thirty minutes of exceptionally varied music, and a musical memory, which needs to be developed with repeated listening and ear training. Helm had ready access to a score, and to successive performances of the late quartets by outstanding ensembles of his time: in his book on Beethoven's quartets he mentions Ferdinand Laub (1832–75) and Joseph Joachim (1831–1907) as excellent quartet leaders.[21] He does not discount the listener, and, among others but unlike Wagner, considered the visual experience of instrumental performance to be important.[22] But his analysis of Op. 131 still presupposes professional performers, connoisseur listeners, and silent, attentive listening.

AFTER HELM: LISTENING FOR UNITY

Wagner's description of Op. 131's inner coherence in terms of Christian imagery was influential, but less so than Helm's observation about thematic recall. Edward Dannreuther, who translated many of Wagner's writings including his *Beethoven* essay (London, 1880), emphasized the spiritual interpretation: in the music of the third period, Beethoven "touches upon the domain of the seer and the prophet . . . he delivers a message of religious love and resignation" so that "each work is in the full sense of the term a revelation."[23] And Joseph de Marliave (1925) married the thematic connection between Nos. 1 and 7 with Wagner's affective interpretation, describing a "melancholy cast" connecting this theme in the finale and the overall mood of No. 1.[24] But over the next decades discussion of the expressive content of the work was generally dropped as new formalist analysis took hold. In analysis after Hugo Riemann (who wrote during the 1880 and 1890s) the quest for inner coherence was grounded in harmonic-motivic aspects, with a heavy emphasis on sonata form. In 1967 Kerman quoted Wagner in passing, but then preferred to draw on Donald Francis Tovey (1927), noting that "Wagner's frame of reference causes alarm nowadays."[25] Wagner's appeal to extra-musical inspiration was the cause of concern.

Building on Helm's analysis of thematic unity in Op. 131, Tovey (1927) made extensive and influential observations on formal coherence and tonal unity.[26] In his essay "On Beethoven's Art Forms," the C-sharp minor quartet is singled out as "outwardly the most abnormal of all his larger works."[27] Yet Tovey argues that the work's apparent freedoms are superficial; they relate to deeper continuity and unity, and ultimately to normality.[28] Beethoven divided Op. 131 into seven "pieces" ("Stücke"), in his terminology, giving each a number (Nos. 1–7).[29] Up to that point, by far the most common macro structure for a string quartet was four movements, the *quatuor brillant* and *quatour concertant* often containing three or even two movements. Helm had suggested that Op. 131's seven parts actually equated to five movements. Now Tovey fits the seven parts into the four that are "normal" in traditional string quartet composition: Nos. 1 and 2 are a conjoined opening sonata form; No. 3 comprises "eleven bars of declamatory interlude," and No. 6 is sidelined as "the introduction to the finale."[30] Other scholars, notably Lewis Lockwood in 2005, took up this regrouping of movements.[31]

Tovey's finding of tonal normality throughout Op. 131 was also influential. Even though the tonal areas and transitions are often unexpected, Tovey argues that the keys are actually related; but his survey of keys "heard in the course of the work" is selective, omitting those that do not relate to the movements or functions he considers important.[32] Picking up this idea two years later, Vincent d'Indy found that the whole quartet is tonally organized on the plan of a cadence.[33] And in 1995 Leonard Ratner showed how the entire tonal plan is motivated by a movement to keys on the flat side of C minor in No. 1: "This single circumstance—a deep descent into subdominant regions—sets the harmonic direction for the entire quartet. It is followed by a rise to the fifth above the home key just before the finale."[34] Again, this builds on Tovey, who was particularly struck by the unifying effect in Op. 131 of the recall of the Neapolitan move from No. 1 in No. 7, and at the recapitulation of the second subject. Tonally now, as well as thematically, "the wheel has come full circle." "The whole quartet is a perfect unity," writes Tovey, "governed by the results of the initial event of the modified first movement which maintained itself in the flat supertonic after the opening fugue had firmly established the key of C sharp minor."[35]

Thematic connections across Opp. 130–133 had been pointed out by Paul J. Bekker (1911), in an elaborate comparison.[36] Mid-twentieth-century commentators like Daniel Gregory Mason (1949) were influenced by Bekker, and still essentially following Helm. Mason speaks of the opening fugue's "germinal subject." This opening fugue, rather than Op. 133, is properly the "great fugue," he finds, "so wide is the span of its conception that many of its details refer far beyond themselves *and beyond it*, some of them becoming fully explicable only in the light of the whole Quartet."[37] But now Tovey's insistence on *tonal* unity throughout the quartet had taken hold in the discussion of the work's unity. Mason and Kerman both stress the recall of the Neapolitan in the finale, Mason pointing to the "deep D major glow" and our discovery of the "structural rightness" of this.[38] He assumed that his listeners had what Tovey calls "Beethoven's long-distance feeling for tonality."[39]

But even a striking move to the Neapolitan in the finale of Op. 131 is difficult to hear after five intervening pieces in diverse keys, however carefully planned and internally restricted. Like long-range thematic connections, perception of tonal links depends on a kind of concentration and recall that is developed only with repetition and expertise. Kerman describes the thematic recall in the finale as a "clear, indeed blatant, functional reference to the theme of another movement," a recall that is "so much of an assault that some competent listeners have refused to believe their ears."[40] He cites J. W. N. Sullivan (1927), who seems, however, to have found the recall oblique rather than blatant: "the character of the theme, as it occurs [in No. 7], is entirely changed, and any symbolic significance it may have is not obvious."[41] Robert Winter comments on the "scrambling" permutations of the opening notes, which cost Beethoven a good deal of thought as he integrated them into the finale.[42] Arguably the thematic recall and the tonal connections *become* clear to many dedicated listeners, emerging as the finale progresses, but perhaps only during repeated listening to the work.

Tovey, to be fair, recognizes listeners in his "Art Forms" essay: he acknowledges at the outset that verbal descriptions cannot substitute for "the music itself"—for listening. The "naïve listener," in possession of "the right musical sensations," becomes a connoisseur through repeated listening.[43]

The *emergent* character of listening experience should be underscored here, in two respects. On the one hand there is the individual listener, listening attentively and perhaps repeatedly until contours and connections become clear. Simultaneously, and over a much larger time scale, there is the accumulating documentation and analysis including listening to recordings. Recordings of Beethoven's quartets became available in Tovey's time, although opportunities to listen to Op. 131 played professionally were still uncommon. This collective knowledge does not necessarily contribute to clarify the listening process, although it doubtless informs it. Mason points out that even the best recordings sometimes obscured subtleties, citing those of the Budapest and Busch Quartets, both of which would have been known to Tovey.[44] Of course, reading analyses of a work can also clarify and direct the way one listens, so that new layers of meaning emerge over time. But the question remains: to whom does the normality and unity of Op. 131, which Tovey and others are at pains to demonstrate, actually become apparent, and when? How much has criticism directed the art of listening to the point where listening itself is complicit in creation?

Such questions remained unaddressed in scholarly discourse until the twenty-first century. Kerman, analyzing the finale in 1967, crystallized the view that had been emerging in the twentieth century. Op. 131 is normal, he finds, because it recalls, realizes, and perfects the middle-period style defined by the Fifth Symphony:[45]

In fact, the mood of the C-sharp-minor Finale heightens and purifies the famous C-minor mood of Beethoven's early years.

The great accomplishment lies in preserving all the force and innocence and heroic thrust while discounting any suspicion of overextension of feeling. When Beethoven finally rises to the pretensions of the C-minor mood, they are no longer pretensions. This is another index of the essential normality of the Quartet in C-sharp minor.[46]

In this "middle-period-style" reading of Op. 131, the finale now became a weighty culmination point, which solves all the problems posed by the preceding movements and seals in the unity of the work. Mason finds that Beethoven was "withholding" traditional sonata form until No. 7, "reserving it to ennoble there the structure and crown the expression of the whole . . . the tying of all the knots."[47] Two years later, Kerman would make this same point even more forcefully in a chapter titled "Dissociation and Integration," where Op. 130 represents dissociation and Op. 131 integration. He underscores continuity and resolution in the C-sharp minor quartet: "If we keep the notion of a 'problem,' [the finale of Op. 131] is Beethoven's most nearly perfect solution; if we do not, it simply ranks as his greatest finale . . . the Finale has to deal not only with its own conflicts, but those of the quartet as a whole."[48] He sets out to show how Beethoven builds up to sonata form during the work, so that in the finale we hear not only local tonal and thematic resolution, with the recall of the opening tetrachord idea and Neapolitan move, but finally formal resolution, with the first fully-fledged sonata form in the work.

However, both writers also describe passages in the finale in terms that cast doubt on any such final resolution. Mason speaks of "tying . . . all the knots" in the sense of resolving problems, but he also describes the "final spiritual triumph" in terms of paradox rather than resolution: "the sudden transitions and extraordinary contrast by which [Beethoven] now confronts grim resolution with fathomless suffering, and this again with noble aspiration and the final spiritual triumph which yet remains tragic."[49] Kerman's descriptions also undermine his claim of resolution. He narrates the opening of the finale in the language of violence and physicality, and like Mason he is struck by sharp contrasts in the coda: "Between rapture and pathos, between extremes of exaltation and tragic grief, the coda rages back and forth from one matchless inspiration to another."[50] In Kerman's account, ambiguity in the finale turns abruptly into a force for coherence: "the whole scene clouds over ambiguously with subdominant harmony; and this ambiguity simply provides the last great binding force of organic interrelation."[51] As to the diverse character of the six preceding pieces, he agrees with Tovey that they are inherently "flat," largely devoid of the inner conflicts and modulations expected in this idiom, thus loading on to the finale a huge dramatic significance. After the fact, presumably, we hear each of the preceding pieces yield up part of its autonomy "in the interest of the work as a whole."[52] Ultimately the quartet is "about" continuity: "Every aspect of this amazing work serves mutually with every other."[53] In sum, there was a strong tradition of seeking and finding unity in the scholarship on Op. 131 up to the late twentieth century.

Thirty-three years later, in a completely different analytical climate, Kerman reversed his views on Op. 131. His new reading reflects an intervening crucial phase in music criticism, profoundly influenced by critical thinkers of the early to mid-twentieth century, including the Frankfurt school and Theodor W. Adorno in particular. Adorno famously analyzed the *Missa Solemnis* as a "late work without late style"; but he mentioned in passing several other such works in his notes, among them Op. 131, for an unfinished Beethoven book.[54] Like Kerman, Helm and others, he probably heard "middle-period" traits in Op. 131; but whereas they found these traits praiseworthy, Adorno would find them problematic. For him the "late style" proper represents Beethoven's overthrowing of conventions and all they represent—not tying up all the knots with a finale in traditional sonata form. In particular, late style for Adorno undoes Viennese classicism: "It is as if Viennese classicism, combined from the 'learned' and the 'gallant,' were polarized again into its elements: the spiritualized counterpoint and the unsubliminated, *un*assimilated 'folksiness.'"[55]

For some listeners, though, this account of late style might equally describe Nos. 1 and 2 from Op. 131. In 2000 Kerman decided that Adorno was wrong to exclude Op. 131 from the late style; contrary to his own 1967 analysis, he set out to show how the finale especially is characterized by *dis*continuity and lack of resolution.[56] He remains fixed on Helm's motivic recall, which he now calls "retrieval." But now, like Sullivan, he recognizes a certain slipperiness or ambiguity of meaning, and finds the way the finale's second theme works on the listener insidious: "The conjunction of augmented second and augmented fourth nags at our ears again and again as the music proceeds."[57] This seems to turn the theme into something like the "Sprüche" (sayings) of fairy tales; the recall, with its continuation, "has been meticulously crafted to make it aberrant, eccentric, grotesque."[58] The music has something of the ogre about it; it is uncanny.

LISTENING AND "MASTER SCENARIOS"

It is a pity that Kerman did not elaborate on the uncanny element in Op. 131—how it is invoked, and how it might affect listeners. He seems to have been intent on showing that the work does conform to Adorno's understanding of late style, rather than exploring what this might mean for various listeners. Like Tovey, Kerman is well aware of the listener, and of the way analytical discourse in presuming to speak for listeners also influences them. In his 1994 article on "Close Readings of the Heard Kind," Kerman carries out a similar re-reading, this time of Beethoven's String Quartet in F minor, Op. 95, making a case for it as a "late work" that invokes the uncanny. He reacts to Lawrence Kramer and others who find that music analysts tend to automatically "reproduce the mastery scenario," presuming to speak for a composer and also to legislate what the music means to "us."[59] Kerman claims that Gary Tomlinson is wrong in proposing that we may never escape from "master scenarios."[60] But he never actually shows how. Replacing a reading of Op. 131 in terms of unity with one that celebrates the work in terms of Adorno's "late style" is not a solution. After all, Adorno's "late style" is also a brand of master scenario: in Adorno's telling, the disruptions and violent vacations of the late style result in the most authentic of all of Beethoven's music, which leaves behind Viennese classicism and carves out a space for Beethoven's own authorial signature in his music.[61]

Some more recent scholars are trying to move away from master scenarios for Op. 131 by including the listener, the experiencing subject, in their analyses, and allowing for multiple modes of listening, including historically-informed listening. Kinderman, for example, disputes Adorno's understanding of the late style as applied to the five late quartets. He places these works on the "threshold to a new creative period," and finds that they simply do not conform to the aesthetics of disruption, as Adorno would have it.[62] Instead he understands this new period in productive and generative terms, where the aesthetics of Jean Paul (Richter) are the touchstone and a key category is "non-linear temporality," experienced by the listener as the quartets unfold. In Op. 131, he traces a pattern of one movement "foretelling the next."[63] So the finale still functions as a culmination, but in the paradoxical sense of showing extreme reluctance to allow resolution.[64]

Of all the scholars discussing Op. 131, Gerd Indorf is the only one to invoke listening in a sustained way: he helps us to think about the idea of multiple readings.[65] Like Kinderman, he appeals to ways of thinking and experiencing in Beethoven's day, which yields insights that have bypassed scholars in the Op. 131 analytical tradition. Scholars in this tradition have tended to build on one another's work, and adhere to the analytical paradigms and discursive habits of their own times, colored by their own ideologies and agendas—Wagner representing nationalism and Adorno Marxism, for example. Stepping away from the analytical tradition, Indorf finds that No. 2 has to be understood in terms of the entire quartet, and especially the fugue that precedes it (see Chapter 4). And Amanda Glauert finds that the opening fugue sets up a listening orientation that allows us to hear the entire work as a gradually emerging process (see Chapter 3).[66] These writers suggest that we do not have to accept any one account—one way of listening to the work—in the end.

CHAPTER 2

POPULAR AND EARLY RECEPTION

THERE'S NO SINGLE CORRECT interpretation of musical works. Rather, reception has many facets, some contradictory and several scarcely studied. Who listens to and responds to Beethoven? Most studies of the reception of Western classical music focus on the work of scholars and critics, considering how their responses to particular works change (or sometimes harden into orthodoxy) over time, as demonstrated in Chapter 1.[1] Missing from most of this conversation is any consideration of popular reception, which can reflect more widely held beliefs about a work than scholarly studies, and also tends to reinforce stereotypes.[2] Op. 131 is no exception. This chapter looks at two contemporary examples of popular reception: a film and a TV drama. They reinforce themes of lack, loss, and tragedy,

Beethoven's String Quartet in C-sharp Minor, Op. 131. Nancy November, Oxford University Press.
© Oxford University Press 2021. DOI: 10.1093/oso/9780190059200.003.0003

which are persistent from Wagner onwards. The later reception of Op. 131's tragedy, especially a stereotype at the popular end, contrasts sharply with the early reception of Op. 131, which celebrated fantasy, fecundity, and plenitude, to the point of perceiving an excess. The early reaction fits with Beethoven's own explicit perception that the work lacked nothing of fantasy. In a humorous understatement he remarked to Karl Holz that the work showed "thank God, less lack of fantasy than ever before" (an *Fantasie fehlt's, Gottlob, weniger als je zuvor!*).[3]

OP. 131 AND LACK

Wagner drew an emphatic connection of Op. 131 with lack, painting Op. 131 in a melancholy hue, and setting a tone that persists to the present day. "The longer introductory Adagio," he wrote, "than which probably nothing more melancholy has been expressed in tones, I would designate as the awakening on the morn of a day that throughout its tardy course shall fulfil not a single desire: not one."[4] A rhetoric of lack or deficiency subsequently emerges in scholarly discourse on the C-sharp minor quartet. Tovey described No. 2 from Op. 131 as a sonata form without a development, and for Kerman each movement is "flat."[5] But, as we have seen, writers find the apparent lack redressed by or because of Op. 131, according to their own analytical and hermeneutic terms: having found a deficiency early in the work (lack of sonata form, lack of modulation within movements, lack of traditional thematic development, and so forth), scholars repeatedly find some resolution and unity in the work as a whole, and emphasize the conclusive character of the finale. Wagner's reading of Op. 131 was couched in expressive rather than analytical terms, but it traces a similar contour: the persona expressed in the work (Beethoven as Christ, or Christ-like Beethoven) will ultimately achieve release from melancholy, transcendence, and apotheosis, albeit outside the work and even outside music.

The scholars after Wagner therefore do not actually find the work "lacking" in either technique or expression: rather, they find that, as a way to generate drama, Beethoven makes a compositional use of "lack," which necessarily leads to fulfillment. This analytical narrative (lack leading to fulfillment) can be related to scholars' "emplotment" of Beethoven's work on this particular quartet.[6] In the scholarship on Op. 131, the idea that the work expresses or is about lack is sometimes read as being biographically motivated. Several accounts of Op. 131, such as Kinderman's, begin with a description of Beethoven's distressing situation toward the end of his life:

> Disorder, conflict, and misery of his life were on the ascent just as his artistic development was attaining new heights. The tragic climax in this biography coincided almost exactly with the completion of his splendid Quartet in C-sharp minor: in the middle of the summer 1826, in a desperate act of self-assertion, his beloved nephew Karl attempted suicide.[7]

But rather than directly map this "tragic climax," this desertion of order, peace, and joy, onto the C-sharp minor quartet, the writers who draw on biography emphasize transcendence, standing in awe of the great work that Beethoven nonetheless managed to produce. In Hayden White's terms, accounts of Op. 131—whether or not they are directly linked to biography—often amount to a Romance "plot"; there is a heroic transcendence of the world and its trials, a victory over it, and (at least in Wagner's account) liberation from it.[8]

Others, especially more recent writers, lean toward a tragic understanding of the work, even if they do not construe Beethoven's life as an outright tragedy. In this frame of reference, the perceived "lack" in the work remains unfulfilled, or Beethoven's compositional use of destabilization remains unresolved. Michael P. Steinberg, for instance, reads the finale's C-sharp major close as compounding the work's prevailing sense of tragedy:

> The rate of harmonic change slows, and the tempo itself is reduced to *poco adagio*. In those few slow measures, the Es become E sharps. We are in C-sharp major. The final measures of quick music are also in that key, but they are far from a conventionally triumphant major-mode close to this, the last of Beethoven's great tragedies in music. For that they come too late and too quickly.[9]

Modern-day popular perceptions of the quartet reinforce the idea of tragedy in connection with Op. 131, entrenching a stereotype and encouraging a limited understanding of the work. Episode 9 of the American war drama mini-series *Band of Brothers* (2001), "Why We Fight," represents the work as melancholy to an extent that goes well beyond Wagner, in a radically different socio-political context. The action takes place as a flashback on a day in 1945 during World War II, when US occupying troops are supervising the cleanup of a bombed German village, named Thalem. A string quartet sits amidst the rubble and smoke, playing No. 6 from Op.

FIGURE 2.1   *Band of Brothers* (2001), "Why We Fight," opening scene.

131 (Figure 2.1).[10] Among the grimmest events of the flash-back are concentration camp scenes, in some of which the few survivors are told by the troops that they are too sick to leave their prison. A glimmer of hope is offered at the end of the flashback with news that Hitler has committed suicide—perhaps one wish fulfilled—only to be darkened by the reflection that this has happened years too late.

A distinction needs to be made between the popular reception of the work itself, in live performance or recording, and the reception of a use of it by a single interpreter (the director) in a popular medium where it is incomplete, possibly unidentified and/or unrecognized by a large proportion of the intended audience. In the case of Op. 131's use within *Band of Brothers*, the sound track, extending to diegetic music, will color some viewers' subsequent encounters with the work as a whole; the director's reaction and repurposing is not necessarily representative of popular reception in general. So in this case one can speak of individual "perceptions" rather than "reception."

The matter is quite different when the producers explicitly invoke the quartet, as in the 2012 film *A Late Quartet*. The general idea of lack in connection with Op. 131 is underscored in this film. We glimpse the lives of a fictitious professional New York quartet, The Fugue, as they prepare to perform Op. 131 in what will be their final concert with their founding cellist, who has been diagnosed with Parkinson's Disease. Sequences from the film encourage the audience to understand this work as portraying struggle against various species of lack: of health, of power, of ability to express passion and love, and of time. The use of Op. 131 as a metaphor for life's struggles is overdone and simplistic in this film: Beethoven's personal struggles (with deafness, and with a father who drank) are represented as directly related to the work's modes of expression, unduly and, in my view, wrongheadedly conflating biography and work. And there is an unhelpful emphasis on the metaphor of "playing second fiddle": the metaphorical construction of the second violin's role as subordinate is particularly untrue of this particular quartet (Beethoven himself comments on the "new manner of part writing" in Op. 131; see Chapter 3 for more on the complex part-writing for all instruments).

But, departing from the mainstream view of twentieth-century scholars that the work ultimately depicts heroic triumph, the producers of *A Late Quartet* deploy the quartet in the interests of tragedy. Toward the end the cellist asks: "Was [Beethoven] maybe trying to point out some cohesion, some unity between random acts of life [with op. 131]?" The question is left hanging. The soundtrack stresses unresolved melancholy, drawing on the opening fugue and No. 6 above all: spare, hushed textures; descending melodic

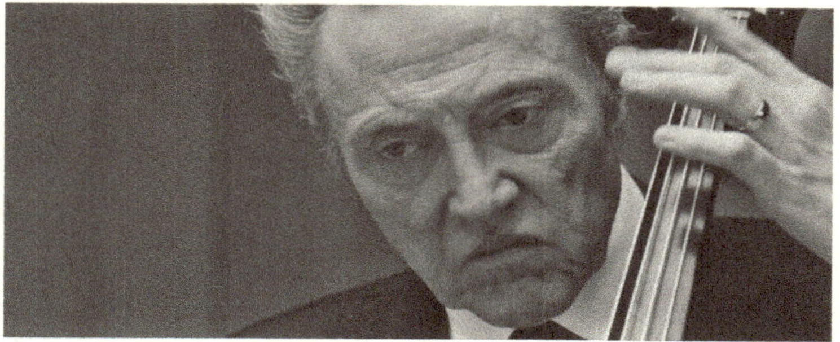

FIGURE 2.2 "It's Beethoven's Fault." Peter Mitchell (Christopher Walken) plays his farewell concert with The Fugue, breaking off before the finale because of its difficulty. No. 7 is especially taxing for the cellist, requiring half position, an advanced cello technique useful for playing music with many flats and sharps.

motion; chromatic harmonies; and awkward intervals. As the film directors interpret it, the finale of Op. 131 certainly does not tie up all the loose ends. The paradox of "unity between random acts of life" places previous readings of cohesion into the darkness of uncertainty, and this film emphasizes that life's random acts entail loss. At the end of the film, Peter breaks off at the finale in a public recital, unable to play further, or indeed to continue his career (Figure 2.2). "It's Beethoven's fault," he says in mock petulance: Beethoven's late work is, apparently, profoundly lacking in sympathy for the performers.

OP. 131 AND PLENITUDE

Reception post-Wagner has tended to find "lack" in the work, understood as eventually resolved or not. A strikingly different perspective emerges in writings by Beethoven and his contemporaries. These commentators speak of plenitude. Composers like Schubert and Schumann, and intellectuals of the time like Adolph Bernhard Marx, heard Beethoven's quartet as full and fecund, and gesturing toward the infinite, bearing out the Romantics' view of the way art works. Of No. 2, Marx writes:

> It is the language of unquenched, endless yearning, which again, as has often been the case, penetrates through from these quartets, which is immediately reflected again in the following "Andante . . . molto cantabile," so full of soul, in an insatiable outpouring of the heart.[11]

Of course "unquenched yearning" and "insatiability" refer by definition to lack—of what is yearned for, and of satisfaction. But this lack itself yields a kind of plenitude, a superfluity of feeling that might overpower the listener. Marx remarked on the plenitude of the late quartets in general and its overwhelming effect on even the expert listener, at least at first. He drew an analogy with the effect of viewing the paintings of Rubens, such as *Lion Hunt* (Figure 2.3):

> Now, this freest unfolding, most delicate design of all four voices discharges a sea of emotions, full of the play of the most variegated, delicate forms, an outpouring rising up from the heart of the singer long alone—separated from humanity in bleak deafness—easily upsetting and confusing the hearer's most receptive, open soul. A similar effect is often brought about by the pictures of Rubens. Confronted by his Lion Hunt or his Sanherib, the more practiced eye needs a while to begin to analyse the abundance of figures and then grasp all the details and the way they are all united in a richly abundant, always consummate whole. Among our poets, it is probably

FIGURE 2.3   Peter Paul Rubens, *The Lion Hunt*, c. 1621. Oil on canvas, 249 cm × 377 cm. (Wikimedia Commons.)

only Heinr. v. Kleist who perhaps gives us a similar image of overflowing emotion, for which no word, no trait, no flood is sufficient.[12]

The reference to the dramatist Heinrich von Kleist (1777–1821) also suggests fecundity of invention. Botstein points out that the parallel could be applied to Kleist's overcharged sources of meaning, feeling, and narrative: "Like a tragic drama, these pieces contained monologues, soliloquies, dialogues, abrupt changes in scene and mood, moments of description, as well as gestures of response, inquiry, and deep meditation."[13]

Composers of the time also transmitted the idea that Op. 131 was "inexhaustible"—leaving nothing be done. Robert Schumann said that Opp. 127 and 131 "have a grandeur . . . which no words can express. They seem to me to stand . . .

on the extreme boundary of all that has hitherto been attained by human art and imagination."[14] Beethoven's own comments are perhaps the most telling. The idea that this work shows "less lack of *imagination* than ever before" needs to be read in the context of his other comments on the late quartets. They take an ironic and mischievous tone, which betrays the composer's excitement about his creative overflow. His remark to Schott that Op. 131 is "patched together from pieces filched here and there" seems to have been provoked by irritation over Schott's request for *original* compositions, but it probably also referred to his compositional methods.[15] Beethoven dispelled the publisher's needless concerns,[16] and elsewhere clarified his creative process: rather like a patchwork of cloth and thread, Op. 131 uses "remainders," which are musical ideas he has developed in the course of writing other works—in this case the other recently composed quartets. Lenz passes on the report of Beethoven's friend and violinist Karl Holz that Beethoven had so many ideas left over from Op. 132 he was more or less impelled to write Opp. 131 and 135:

> During the composing of the three quartets desired by Prince Galitzin (Opp. 127, 130, 132), such a wealth of new quartet ideas flowed from Beethoven's inexhaustible imagination that he almost involuntarily had to write the C sharp minor and F major quartets. "Best [friend], I've already thought of something else!" he used to say jokingly and with shining eyes when we went for a walk: he wrote some notes in his sketchbook. "But this belongs to the second next quartet (C sharp minor), the next one (which means the B flat quartet Op. 130 with 6 movements) already has too many movements."[17]

These comments are a most compelling reason for reading the individual pieces making up Op. 131 in terms of fecundity, rather than "flatness".

Early writers mention the predominantly somber affect of the work, but they do not necessarily read it as an explicit tragedy. For Marx, the opening fugue is "a stranger's plea in misunderstood language; only the tone of the voice, the begging glances, the urge of the soul, we feel—what it desires, what torments it, we do not grasp."[18] A reviewer of 1828 described the work as a "nocturn" in the manner of Rembrandt, surmising that "Beethoven must've been sick of soul when he wrote the work."[19] But then Marx points out that the work is far from uniform in affect. There are, after all, seven pieces in Op. 131, and a share of joy to be heard between them, especially in the finale:

> [Op. 131] betrays what from time to time crept into Beethoven's soul as a premonition, even if occasionally—in the Presto, in the Finale—the original freshness of life full of courage and cheerfulness was restored.[20]

In a footnote, Marx refers to Beethoven's letter to Schott of September 17, 1824, where Beethoven expands on his sense of creative energy and his urgent desire to write abundantly: "Apollo and the muses will not yet let me be delivered to the grim reaper, for I owe them so much and I must leave this before my departure into the Elysian Fields, which gives me the spirit and means to complete it. To me, it is as if I had hardly written anything."[21]

The work's dedication, too, can be related to its prevailing affect. Beethoven chose to dedicate the work to

Baron Joseph von Stutterheim as a gesture of gratitude for taking his nephew, Karl, into the army after Karl's suicide attempt. Of all his personal cares, Karl's welfare was arguably the one that troubled Beethoven most in his final years, as the conversation books reveal. It seems unlikely that Beethoven would have dedicated in relieved gratitude a work expressing mostly darkness and tragedy. Originally, then, the work was understood in a starkly different way from its selective representation in modern-day popular media, especially *Band of Brothers*, where Hitler's suicide actually provides a point of relief from the weary sorrows and infinite pain of military life.

Crucially, there is a distinct positive strand in the early reception of Beethoven's late quartets.[22] Granted, some early listeners found Beethoven's late quartets difficult to understand and therefore to be lacking in meaning, the utterances of a deaf madman. The Belgian François-Joseph Fétis (1784–1871) represents this view. In a long review of Op. 131 for the *Revue musicale* in 1830, he uses Beethoven's deafness to explain the late works' difficulty:

> the natural disposition of his mind made him unsociable; a deplorable infirmity, the most complete deafness, a terrible misfortune for a musician . . . resulted in sequestering him from the world. Does the prolongation of this disability, lasting many years, result in making him forget to some extent the effect of sounds? This is what is likely, if we consider some of the harmonic successions that have been prevalent in his latest productions.[23]

But a belief in the transcendent greatness of the five late quartets was also clearly emerging, and before Wagner. Alexander Oulibicheff writes in his *Beethoven, ses critiques et ses glossateurs* (1857):

> Already we can look forward to the day when the recognition of the last five will leave Op. 59 as far behind as Op. 59 has left Op. 18. Today the Op. 59 are called the "great" Beethoven quartets; soon the Opp. 127, 130, 131 and 135 will be called the "very great."[24]

Oulibicheff was no lone prophet: other critics of Fétis's time challenged contemporary claims that Beethoven's illness and deafness led directly to bizarre anomalies in his late works. In 1828 a reviewer of Op. 131 in the North German music journal *Cäcilia* admonished the listener to try to understand the late works' difficulties. First, the reviewer represented the pathological explanation of the late works as a kindly but lazy way out:

> One believes oneself to be judging the later [quartets of Beethoven] most indulgently if one regards them with consternation, putting off a definite judgement to future times. Those who are most comfortable with this explain candidly, with a fair degree of compassion, that one can see from these later works that the composer, sick in spirit, was incapable of giving the appropriate direction to his ideas.[25]

But then the reviewer moved to praise instead the abundance and variety of ideas and feelings in the challenging works, which he relates to the idea of the poetic genius:

> To them belong all degrees and shadings that spread through this immense domain. Memories of happiness, of composure,

of the most tender, delicate emotion, alternate with the expression of firm seriousness, of deep melancholy, of impetuously excited passion. How the true genius brings all of this to living representation constitutes the incomprehensible, has its foundation in the endlessness of poetic genius,—and this it is that, which in narrow-minded judgements, is called incomprehensible, extravagant.[26]

The writer deploys the rhetoric of plenitude liberally in characterizing Op. 131: the work is profoundly expressive, and exudes novelty and inexhaustibility (*originell, Neuheit, Unerschöpflichkeit*). Implicitly, lazy listeners are admonished to try harder.

Wherever the early reception of Op. 131 was at all positive, the writers tended to emphasize plenitude, along with the deep engagement of the listener. A celebrated critic and long-time editor of the *Allgemeine musikalische Zeitung*, Friedrich Rochlitz (1769–1842), for example, wrote a lengthy review of Op. 131 in 1828. Rochlitz's predominant impression was that the quartet was colorful, whimsical, and spontaneous. His praise is limited: he is clearly wary of the work's sheer originality. But, affirming its deep effect on the listener, he treats it as a massive fantasia, and uses a metaphor of exploration to describe the process of his own listening to it:

[The reviewer] had expected something unusual, indeed strange, but what he now found appeared so motley and irregular, at times so highly singular and arbitrary, that he often did not know what to make of it. The melodies—what could be discerned of them in such isolation—for the most part completely odd, but deeply gripping, even, perhaps, incisive;

  STRING QUARTET IN C-SHARP MINOR

for the most part no continuation or working out of them to be perceived, much less followed, and yet it always seemed to be obscurely present, occasionally breaking out in wonderful ways. The modulations not infrequently pushed to the point of being bizarre—indeed, grating. And so, in every aspect, including outward arrangement (like an overly large fantasy, ever changing and transforming anew) . . . He believed only that he could surmise more than he understood, that the deep shaft, so troublesome to traverse, was as rich in veins of gold as any that Beethoven had discovered and excavated.[27]

The listener is repeatedly confounded by unexpected and strange features that resist complete understanding, he proposes, but also sustained by an elusive, intermittently perceived continuity, and ultimately rewarded with subterranean gold.

LEVELS OF LISTENING

The negative reaction of Fétis compared with Rochlitz may reflect simple nationalist bias on both sides. The French were distinctly slower to accept Beethoven's music than people in the Austro-German lands.[28] And the German, upper-middle class, inevitably male critic had political as well as musical grounds for underscoring the power of Beethoven's music, understood as an exploratory, emancipatory force.[29] But the various reactions of early critics also depended on *who* was playing, and how. Some critics complained that early performances of the late quartets were under-rehearsed, which inhibited assessment. Ignaz von Seyfried makes this point emphatically in another review of Op. 131 in *Cäcilia* (1828).

Unlike the earlier *Cäcilia* reviewer quoted above, he finds the work dark and over-long, and reaches for biography to explain it.[30] But this influential Austrian musician and composer did not want to pass final judgement after only one hearing, of one performance: "The author has heard it only once, and what is more, if by capable artists, yet, being too little acquainted with the composition itself, highly mediocre."[31] Emil Platen conjectures that Seyfried was referring to a private performance by the Schuppanzigh quartet.[32]

Performers of the time, like audiences, were hearing the works for the first time; they were learning, slowly, that they needed to rehearse. In a conversation book from 1825, Holz observed to Beethoven, "we only rehearse your quartets, not those of Haydn and Mozart, [which] work better without rehearsal."[33] It is unclear exactly how thorough the "rehearsals" were in this case, and possible that the violinist was trying to flatter Beethoven. But this piece of evidence and several others shows that extensive rehearsal (and thus repeated listening and kinaesthetic learning on the part of the performers) was not yet the norm. Rochlitz argues at length that the C-sharp minor quartet must be well rehearsed in order to bring it off properly. Seeking "help through his ears," he explains that he invited a quartet society to his house: "thoroughly capable musicians who were also admirably practised together and were all fervent admirers of Beethoven."[34] Rehearsal, ideally combined with score study, was coming to be considered necessary for Beethoven's quartets. Another reviewer of Op. 131 observed that a score is very useful for performers: "We must be aware of great gratitude toward the Schott music firm for making the works of our Beethoven available to us in score, for such works must be studied most urgently by prospective artists. But such a score is likewise very welcome for works that present such great difficulties in performance."[35]

Listeners' reactions also depend on *how* they listen; this is not just a matter of experience and musicality, but also of willingness or frame of mind. This early reception of Op. 131 notably motivates much discussion of listening itself. Early reviewers such as Marx, Rochlitz, Fétis, and Berlioz wrote extended reviews, ostensibly of the work, but they actually say very little about what they heard and much more about *how* they and others listened. In his 1828 review of Op. 131, Rochlitz distinguishes at length two different types of listener, only one of whom is right for late Beethoven:

> We must consider the public as belonging to two most different classes, according to sensibility and inclination, and likewise to number, in regard to music—approximately as in regard to reading matter and to many other things as well. The first only wants to amuse itself with music, whether hearing or practising it—to create an agreeable pastime. The second wants to excite, occupy, reanimate, uplift, strengthen, advance its whole inner person, according to all its powers, and as consistently as possible. To this belongs even, when opportunity presents itself, extending it by learning new things. The first class, in our opinion, will do well to renounce these most recent works of B.[36]

This could be taken for a typical, simplistic division of connoisseur from amateur, but Rochlitz's comments on the amateur complicate the issue. In particular, he explains that his second class of listeners will not comprehend the work straight away: "It should thus be assumed that they will maintain all their powers as far as possible during the performance, and likewise completely surrender themselves to what affects them and in this manner occupies them. But not everything will, or can, affect them and occupy them thus: not, at least, at the first hearing, even with ever so heightened attentiveness."[37] Rochlitz is describing an open frame of mind, allowing deep engagement, and dedication to listening repeatedly. He is also distinguishing various levels of listening, rather than just two types of listener. The first listening by either kind of listener will not entail full attention: the listener will switch in and out of the "deeper" mode of listening. One needs to listen often. Like the reviewer of Schott's editions quoted immediately above, Rochlitz reports the use of a score for study, and notes that scores are necessary to reaching a judgement:

What is more, along with the score, spring had come as well; thus, the man, despite his many reminders, was not yet able to attain the sought-after repetition. He now counted this music, along with the other most recent, peculiar, and at times also singular music of Beethoven, entirely among that which one must have not only read but also heard—and well, and repeatedly—before one can allow a final judgement to be made about it. (And I find that he is right about this.)[38]

Even though Rochlitz finally privileges hearing over score reading here, listening *with* a score directs one's attention to different aspects of the work than are accessible when either listening as a performer of a part or watching as an audience member: structural points, and overall impressions, rather than the moment-by-moment unfolding of form and affect.

Fétis focuses on audience type, and adds a third class of listener, with whom he has little sympathy because he considers them to be posturing:

> An audience gathers to hear Beethoven's last quartets, possibly composed of three kinds of individuals. The first will comprise those who are not insensitive to music, who especially like easy melodies, and who only conceive harmony as the accessory part of art. This class, the largest among those who take the title of music lovers, will absolutely not understand this one [i.e., Op. 131] . . . The second group of listeners will be composed of artists who have made a more or less in-depth study of the various parts of the art, and who will compare what they hear with what they know by acquired wisdom; their ears will be wounded at every moment by inconsistencies of harmony; their attention will be tired by continuous divagations; in vain will they seek some similarity of plan between these whimsical new works and the masterpieces of art, enshrined by the admiration of all ages; they will lack the patience to make the long examination necessary to understand Beethoven's purpose; yet, who can flatter themselves by understanding the music they will not understand? . . . Lovers eager for new things of any kind, enthusiasts of Beethoven's talent, or rather of his name, make up the third class of listeners who one notices at Mr. Bohrer's evenings, where the last quartets of this great artist are performed. They are no more initiated than the others regarding the point of these compositions; but they applaud and swoon anyway.[39]

Berlioz's comments on Op. 131 from around the same time make contrary judgments: Fétis says that those who seem to understand the music are posturing, whereas Berlioz excludes those who do not understand from the elite group of serious, attentive listeners. Berlioz wrote about Beethoven in a journal called *Le Correspondant*, in two articles in August and October 1829. The C-sharp minor quartet was performed by Baillot's quartet:

There were in the room some two hundred people who listened with a religious attention. After a few minutes, there was a sort of malaise in the room; people began talking in low voices, each telling his neighbour that he's bored; eventually, unable to combat such fatigue, nineteen out of twenty of those present got up, saying out loud that it was intolerable, incomprehensible, ridiculous; "it is the work of madman, it is without common sense," etc. . . . in one corner of the room I found a little group (and I need hardly say I was part of it, whatever anyone says) whose feelings and thoughts were quite different. The members of this almost invisible fraction of the public, well anticipating the effect performing the new quartet would have on most other people, were gathered together so that their listening could be undisturbed. After a few bars of the first movement, I began to fear that I'd be bored, without, however, allowing my concentration to lose its intensity. Quite soon this disorder seemed to resolve itself; just when the patience of the mass of the public was running out, mine was aroused and the composer's genius became accessible. Imperceptibly, it strengthened; I felt an unfamiliar tremble in my circulation, my arterial pulsation accelerated, and from the second movement, which follows the first without a break, frozen with astonishment, I turned to one of my neighbours and saw his face was pale, and sweating; the others were still as statues. Bit by bit, a heavy weight seemed to press on my breast as in a horrible nightmare, I felt my hair tingling, my teeth chattering, all my muscles contracting and finally, in a part of the finale, given extreme force by Baillot's energetic bowing, I shed cold tears; tears of anguish and terror, fell from my eyes and marked the climax of this cruel emotion.[40]

Again, the behavior of audiences and musical demeanor of performers heard by Fétis and Berlioz might have influenced their very different views of Op. 131. An anonymous report from Berlin in the April 1830 volume of *Berlin allgemeine musikalische Zeitung* praised the German Bohrer Quartet for *not* exhibiting the first-violin-centric behavior that had characterized Pierre Baillot's quartet concerts in Paris.[41] So it is possible that Berlioz had heard a more first-violin-centric performance than had Fétis. But Mary Hunter notes that around this time German critics could stoop to pointing out what they considered to be pervasive failures in French performance practice.[42] It is also possible that German critics were simply inclined to be unfairly tougher on French performers and generally find French performance wanting because French.

In most cases, then, opinions of the work depend on various factors: who was speaking (critic, composer); national allegiances (French, German); who was playing and how (well-rehearsed or not, equally-balanced or first-violin-centric), and perhaps most importantly the speaker's ideology of listening. The date of Berlioz's review, 1829, is striking: he had recently failed to gain the Prix de Rome, because his music was considered disordered, rather the way the "mass of the public," in Berlioz's term, allegedly thought of Beethoven. In some respects Berlioz represents his own conception of the ideal "romantic listener": one who "feels" the work (and would thus understand his own work) deeply, physically, and personally—in isolation from the sentiments of the masses.

Fétis had his own politics of listening, which was related to his background, and in several ways quite the opposite to that of Berlioz. He was among the conservative professors at the Paris Conservatoire who represented the establishment, whereas Berlioz represented the individual, blazing his own fresh path in the wake of revelations such as Beethoven's music. Of Berlioz, Fétis wrote: "what Monsieur Berlioz composes is not part of that art which we distinguish as music, and I am completely certain that he lacks the most basic capability in this art." Fétis was not, primarily, seeking the understanding of an elite old school as a composer (and probably also trying to improve the taste of the wider audience). He was a writer on music and a critic who wanted to reach out to a large audience and make music understandable. For example, one of his projects was an enormous compilation of biographical data in the *Biographie universelle des musiciens*. He tended to talk in terms of historical trajectories and what we might call big pictures. Liberty, equality, and fraternity were his touchstones, not elitist values and obscure "high art."

And as for the term "fantastique"—so widely applied to Beethoven's Op. 131, so fundamental to Berlioz's *Symphonie Fantastique*—Fétis was sourly dismissive: "this word has even slid into music. 'Fantastique' music is composed of instrumental effects with no melodic line and incorrect harmony."[43] But Fétis was fighting the tide of musical taste in this respect. Beethoven and others of the time explicitly valued *Fantasie* greatly. In his terms the C-sharp minor quartet was the high point of all the late quartets in terms of the length and diversity of *Fantasie*, and in that sense it was also of a piece with those late works. We see this in early reception, and Beethoven acknowledged to Karl Holz, cited above, that the work came in a stream of inspiration that flowed from one late quartet to the next.[44]

CHAPTER 3

"A NEW KIND OF PART WRITING"

He had first received it engraved in parts . . . he spread the parts out next to one another, certainly not hoping thereby to become exactly familiar with the work—to master it—but rather to instruct himself about its essence, its purpose, its construction, and its manner . . . [1]

THIS IS ROCHLITZ, REFERRING to himself in the third person in his 1828 review of Op. 131. He describes his immediate impulse to *look* at the music for a first impression. The work was supplied in its most readily available form, four performance parts; so he spread them out to explore the "gold mine," as he put it, visually, before seeking performers to further his understanding of the work. While the score and parts of Op. 131 certainly offer a window onto

Beethoven's String Quartet in C-sharp Minor, Op. 131. Nancy November, Oxford University Press.
© Oxford University Press 2021. DOI: 10.1093/oso/9780190059200.003.0004

the work's construction, Rochlitz maybe asks too much of them: experiencing the work in performance using sight and physical sensation as well as hearing, is arguably vital for understanding its purpose and manner, and particularly its "essence."

Nevertheless, the engraved parts might have given him a tantalizing glimpse of the novelty of its construction. This chapter explores the "new kind of part writing" that Beethoven claimed for Op. 131, from his compositional perspective, and from that of contemporary performance and reception. Part-writing analysis is facilitated by looking and feeling as well as listening: looking at how themes and motives are shared and "played out" in performance, and feeling the changing sonorities, physically, helps understanding of Beethoven's multi-faceted manipulation of the quartet soundscape. Robin Wallace finds that in Beethoven's middle period "he showed the most notable musical response to his growing deafness, emphasizing features that could be *felt physically* by the performers and challenging his listeners' auditory imaginations with textures that *appealed to the eyes* as well as to the ears."[2] These auditory challenges are still more pronounced in the late quartets, especially Op. 131, where they cry out for a holistic way of hearing.

NEW PART WRITING?

Helm quotes Holz's report of Beethoven claiming that the late quartets employ "a new kind of part writing (meaning the instrumentation, the distribution of roles)."[3] The report comes to us third-hand, but what he says about part writing fits with the view of string quartet composition prevailing since the mid-eighteenth century and continuing to develop in Beethoven's time.[4] It makes it clear that Beethoven had a specific interest in part writing for the quartet, but might leave us wondering what room was left for innovation in this area by 1826. Motivic and thematic development (*thematische Arbeit*) were recognized as vital in the string quartet; but *equality* between the parts in motivic development, specifically, was held to be central to the "true" quartet. Johann Conrad Wilhelm Petiscus exemplifies this way of thinking in an extended article "On Quartet Music" for the *Allgemeine musikalische Zeitung* (1810):

> It appears to us an essential aspect of the true quartet that all four voices unite in an inseparable whole through like participation in the *main melodic material* of the piece. This occurs *simultaneously* in two ways: the main melodic idea of the tone-painting (possibly in different versions) is alternately taken up and expressed by the different voices—alterna amant Camoenae[5]—and, in alternation with the above, a multi-part song can be discerned, in which all the voices progress melodically. It is chiefly the latter that constitutes the character of the true quartet.[6]

In fact fugue, in which the equality of the four voices is very obvious, had long been held to be the ideal quartet texture. For the earliest theorists of the quartet in North Germany in the mid-eighteenth century, good quartet writing meant skilled counterpoint. Even in the 1790s, the influential theorist Heinrich Christoph Koch still spoke of the ideal quartet in terms of fugal textures, while advising that a mixture of styles was necessary for quartets in the modern style of composers like Haydn and Mozart.[7] Four-part fugue of the kind Koch meant remained an ideal for string quartets into the early nineteenth century. Petiscus's comments reflect this norm. The ideal of four equal voices in the string quartet can also be seen, for example, in an 1808 review in the *Allgemeine musikalische Zeitung* of string quartets by Florian Leopold Gassmann and Matthias Georg Monn, which had been reprinted in Vienna in 1804, around thirty years after their composition. The reviewer praised Gassmann's fugal Allegros, and noted the thematic working that pervades all four voices in the slow movements and minuets, concluding that "these compositions deserve the title Quatuor [Quartet] in the strictest sense of the word."[8] Marx was still drawing on the same model when, in 1828, he mentioned J. S. Bach's counterpoint in connection with Beethoven's late quartets.[9]

"Equality" of part writing was not just a theoretical ideal, but a principle borne out in the string quartets of Beethoven, his predecessors, and his contemporaries. It is remarkable that these composers had not exhausted the possibilities for distributing the roles among the instruments long before Beethoven's late quartets. Haydn's C major quartet, Op. 20, No. 2 (1772) is an early example in which register and role form the main topics for the opening movement.[10] And the varied fugal finales in Haydn's string quartets Op. 20 are high points of sustained fugal writing for quartet.[11]

In the late eighteenth century there was a growing sense that the string quartet genre balanced the desires of connoisseur (listener or performer) with those of amateurs (especially amateur performers, as access to quartet music improved). Amateurs wanted more "conversational" textures, involving more variety and less "equality" (and consequent difficulty) for all the players (never mind listeners).[12] So movements like the finale of Mozart's K. 387 balance fugue and homophony, although contemporary critics typically found the "Haydn'" quartets more to the taste of the connoisseur.[13] If the balance tipped too far toward simple textures with simple melodic sharing, critics like Petiscus found the quartet in question wanting.

Beethoven achieved many landmarks in quartet part writing, and specifically "equality," before Op. 131. Op. 18, No. 1 has much part sharing, especially pronounced in the opening movement. But the third movement of Beethoven's String Quartet in A major Op. 18, No. 5 is perhaps the most relevant instance: within a variations movement that otherwise closely follows the opening of the third movement of Mozart's String Quartet in A major, K. 464, Beethoven unexpectedly inserts a cheeky fugue, in a bold move in which contemporary listeners could hear one-upmanship toward Mozart.[14] In other words, early in his career as a quartet composer, Beethoven was already using fugue within a string quartet to make his mark in the genre by challenging a venerable tradition. Such developments continue in Op. 59, No. 1, with prominent fugal working in contrast to "free" writing in the development section of the first movement. But for an entire fugal movement, the closest to Op. 131 is the Grosse Fuge, which was originally intended as a massive fugal finale for the String Quartet in B flat, Op. 130.

So the ideal of "equality" of voices in quartet part writing was not new, and quartet composers worked with it in numerous ways long before Beethoven's late quartets. Most commentators agree that the quartets of Haydn, Mozart,

Beethoven, and other "connoisseur" quartets of the era contain thematic working-out in which all voices have some share in the development of themes. Scholars from the late nineteenth century onwards have sought to locate the advent of the "true" or (more recently) "Classical" quartet, usually at a point well before 1826 and Op. 131: in Haydn's six quartets Op. 33 of 1781, which he claimed were written "in a completely new and special manner."[15] James Webster shows how this claim is taken up in scholarship on "Classical style" (and "Classical string quartets" in particular) from the late nineteenth century onwards. Narrating in effect an archetypal Romance plot, Adolf Sandberger (1934) was the first of several commentators to construe Haydn's Op. 33 as the turning point in the creation of Classical style:

> Now the master takes up quartet composition again [after a ten-year gap or "crisis" since Op. 20] and writes [Op. 33] "*in an entirely new and special manner*" . . . The principle of motivic development has taken possession of the string quartet; *the modern string quartet is invented* . . .[16]

In practice, Hunter has shown, real equality was rare in the string quartet in the period in question—in composition or in performance.[17] "Equality" of part writing was a matter of ideology, with political and social overtones as well as musical ones. Petiscus, for example, is strongly anti-French, and his comment on "galant" writing betrays his hope of reforming the fashionable French-influenced tastes of the day. Thus it is a moot point as to when the "true" quartet was realized.[18] But a compositional ideal of four-part equality can be inferred, functioning in a regulative capacity, as a benchmark for composers to aspire to and critics to apply. Haydn's string quartets, together with Mozart's (especially his "Haydn" Quartets), were consistent touchstones, and Beethoven's were also cited more and more often. Talking about revisions to Op. 18, No. 1, Beethoven told his friend Karl Amenda in 1801 that he had only just "learnt how to write quartets properly"; this attests to an ideal of quartet writing to which Beethoven aspired.

Beethoven's reference to a "new kind of part writing" in the late quartets—a loaded remark made privately in the 1820s—also suggests aspiration toward an ideal. He then made a loaded and public statement by offering a fugue as the opening movement in Op. 131: this was very first time a composer had written a full fugue as the first movement in a classical string quartet. If Berlioz's listener typology regarding late Beethoven quartets is accurate (see Chapter 2), then, in Paris at least, the fugal opening of Op. 131 was an aural shock that few of the audience would hear in full. They would have expected an opening sonata-allegro movement or similar, with at most a slow introduction by way of complication (as in Mozart's String Quartet in C major, K. 465, "The Dissonance," for example). But now Beethoven's opening fugue in C-sharp minor provided few if any of the formal signposts that listeners expected. Drabkin points out that fugue by its nature lacks such signposts: "the theory of fugue can tell us little about the overall design of a fugue with a beginning, middle, and end," and he echoes Tovey's point that "fugue is a texture, not a form."[19] Indeed, before Op. 131, fugue was associated mainly with closing in the string quartet, as in the fugal finale, or with thematic development within a movement. An opening fugue sent confusing messages.

But as an opening gambit in a string quartet, fugue can set the tone for equality in part writing. Op. 131 follows through rigorously and variously on this promise, which perhaps explains why Beethoven regarded it as his greatest quartet.[20] Modern-day performers have noted the sustained demands this work places on every single member of the ensemble, and the team-work required to bring it off. Additional demand creates an elevated experience for performers. The second violinist of the Colorado Quartet, Deborah Lydia Redding, finds that the parts of Beethoven's late quartets are composed more or less equally, "which leads to some great second violin moments, melodies straight from Beethoven's heart, injected into my bloodstream."[21] And the Prazák Quartet's violist, Josef Kluson, describes the "intense" experience of performing Op. 131; he cites the transition to No. 6, an exhilarating unison crescendo beginning "sul ponticello" (with all players bowing near the bridges of their instruments), as the most fulfilling: "I almost forget I am a violist."[22] This theme of forgetting self in service of the whole recurs through discourse about string quartet performance, and especially regarding this quartet.[23] The violist of the Brooklyn Rider Quartet, Nicholas Cords, says that in Op. 131 "Beethoven asks us to rise to our full potential, to question what it means to be human . . . to experience *a sense of catharsis together*." He recalls: "We spent time together imagining these phrases as a chorus of voices."[24] The Fry Street Quartet's first violinist, Wilhelm Fedkenheuer, observes that the players need to develop agile listening, so as to hear and manipulate their own parts in relation to a whole that can change "lightning speed."[25]

As an opening statement, fugue offers more than the promise of equality in part writing. It is not just a texture in which all voices get an "equal" share, but also one in which all voices have vital and variable roles in the *working out* of themes. In this sense, fugue is a process. Amanda Glauert describes the opening fugue this way: "[It] establishes a new mode of perception which prepares for an understanding of the quartet as a whole: rather than listening for prescribed landmarks, one is led by the slowly unfolding fugal texture to concentrate on the gradual emergence of process."[26] The fugue, with its kaleidoscopically shifting permutations of themes, developed across all voices, sets the mode for the entire work, and especially the variations at its center. Glauert notes that Wagner was inspired by Op. 131 when working on *Das Rheingold*, the opening prelude of which is a 136-bar chord on E flat; there, practically all the formal and tonal signposts expected of an overture are absent and the listener is asked to listen to the prelude as an unfolding creative process.[27] Berlioz, listening to Op. 131, seems to appreciate this point—recording his moment-by-moment reactions to it.

HOLISTIC HEARING

To explore what Beethoven meant by a "new kind of part writing" in connection with Op. 131, we can trace evidence of his process of conceptualizing and writing down the four parts. His sketches and notes relating to the middle-period quartets show a new approach to four-part writing emerging. In particular, there is a note about composing and hearing all four parts at once, which he made in the sketchbook Landsberg 5 around the time he was composing the String Quartet in E-flat major, Op. 74 ("The Harp," c. 1809): "the best way to become practised in composition, about which one speaks or thinks, is to write it out."[28] This fascinating note to self is evidence that composition was an embodied process of learning for Beethoven: it is as if the pen strokes themselves were a physical means of "becoming practised." Writing out as a process of thinking, and especially thinking in four parts, seems to have become more important to him around this time. Regarding Op. 74, Seow-Chin Ong notes: "the second movement sketches in Landsberg 11 are laid out in many instances in 2-part score with four voices." He offers this is evidence of Beethoven's "increasing tendency to think out his music in contrapuntal terms."[29]

These new ways of compositional thinking and working become especially clear with the late quartets, particularly Op. 131. More than 650 pages of sketches and drafts survive for Op. 131, apart from the autograph score, which itself contains numerous revisions, especially of the variations of No. 4. But *score* sketches for Op. 131, that is sketches in several parts, have survived in far greater numbers than those for any other late quartet: almost 200 leaves, which probably represents less than the total number. Beethoven also developed a new method of viewing the quartet as a whole, drawing up synoptic plans that Robert Winter terms "tonal overviews." They reveal how he weighed up the sequence and balance of pieces,[30] and they suggest that he let his sense of sight guide his ear into deep layers of invention.

Beethoven's compositional process was changing with his increasing deafness: he came to rely more and more on the senses of sight and touch, which inform what one hears in ways that we normally do not perceive. In fact, a vast amount of interpretation is carried out by the mind in order to make sense of what we hear, combining data from many sources.[31] Robin Wallace says in his pathbreaking study of Beethoven and deafness: "What you hear is inseparable from where you are and what your mind and *your other senses* tell you about your surroundings."[32] Early in his career, Beethoven started to draw substantially on senses other than hearing in his compositional process. He became accustomed to using the physical act of writing out music, and the visual appearance of his scores, not just to record musical ideas but to generate and develop them.[33] As his deafness increased, and certainly by the time he was composing his last quartets, he came to rely heavily on these physical and visual components of musical invention.[34]

Wallace asks a radical question: "is it possible that the extraordinary creativity of his middle and late periods took place not despite his deafness but because of it?"[35] This is not a new question: Wagner had asked and answered it with an emphatic "Yes" in his Beethoven essay of 1870. But Wagner and Wallace are poles apart in their explanations. Wagner says that Beethoven became *cut off* from the world of appearances and the auditory "noise" around him, which allowed him to carry out inner listening, and thus produce masterpieces of pure sound. Wallace, on the other hand, says that Beethoven became *highly attuned* to the various cues around him, and stored them up along with recollections from his hearing past, in order to "hear" in a richly contextual and refined way; the resulting works are deeply multivalent and require very complex, multi-faceted listening: "As his failing ears increasingly forced his eyes into the driver's seat, he created new musical textures and new approaches to musical form, forever changing the experience of music for those who came after him."[36]

So Beethoven was drawing on the multiple facets of listening (some non-aural) not just to help him compose, but also to invest new meaning in his works. Wallace examines Beethoven's works that demonstrate such a heightened, holistic way of hearing. It is no accident that the works he explores in depth are string quartets, Op. 59 and Op. 133. There is a heightened interest in register in Op. 59, which relates to the visual display involved in performing these works, especially the leaps between high and low registers, which entail string crossing and are readily visible to the audience. Embodied meanings arise, too, for example through the sustained use of the penetrating high register or the resonant lowest strings, which are physically palpable and also easily seen in performances. And these techniques receive redoubled attention in the late quartets—hence the physicality of the quartet-playing experience noted by modern-day performers of Op. 131.

Beethoven was not just invoking other senses as sources of meaning for these works; he was also playing with the process of listening altogether. The manipulation is heightened in the late quartets, and especially Op. 131. He shows that he understands how the ear can distinguish two parts from one complex line, as in the fugue subject of Op. 133. And in Op. 131 the listening game he plays is even more complex. In particular, he challenges the listener to follow a single auditory event that is the product of a more complex, four-part texture, as he works it out in various permutations. He had explored in detail the "classic" quartet texture, in which a single idea gets passed or split between all four voices, in the opening movement of Op. 74; now this idea of splitting a musical figure between the four voices is taken to a completely new level and becomes thematic in Op. 131, especially in No. 4: it amounts indeed to a new kind of part writing.

Timbre also contributes to the complexity and novelty of this kind of part writing. The splitting and sharing of ideas between the four instruments means that the listener must resolve auditory events that are remote in terms of space and timbre. The instruments of a string quartet are sometimes assumed to be homogeneous in terms of timbre, since all are members of the violin family, but in fact they are not. Each member of the violin family possesses its own distinct tone color; and there are subtle changes in timbre across the instruments' various registers, noted by Beethoven's contemporaries, which compound the differences in timbre.[37] The manner of playing also affects timbre, which Beethoven exploits in Op. 131; this applies obviously to pizzicato vs. bowing, but also to the particular manner of bowing (sul ponticello, non ligato, and so on).[38] Distinguishing timbral differentiation is a particularly complex aspect of hearing, so Beethoven probably relied heavily on his eyes and memory to guide him in combining the quartet voices to create new timbres. Perhaps this is why there were so many revisions of the variations in No. 4.

Variation of timbre appropriately follows from Beethoven's intent upon auditory disruption in Op. 131.

Performers have to concentrate hard on ensemble, listening to how their parts fit into the whole; similar demands are made on the listener, who must repeatedly make new connections between parts and rethink the relationships between them. This applies across the quartet, and strikingly in the eleven-bar Allegro moderato, No. 3. The first violin has the ornamental flourish toward the end, but all the voices contribute to creating the voice we hear,

EXAMPLE 3.1   Beethoven, String Quartet in C-sharp minor Op. 131, No. 3, Allegro moderato. Copyright G. Henle Verlag, Munich. Used with permission.

in a shared recitative (Example 3.1). There is dizzying splitting and sharing of melodies and motives in the Presto, because of the sheer speed at which one has to try to synthesize the split theme. A ping-pong effect begins in bar 25: a fragment of the theme (the leap of a fourth), rhythmically altered, is passed down between the four voices; then once again, the leap altered to a major third; and a third time, again rhythmically altered, and slower, more quietly, and condensed to a minor third. All this takes place within just eleven bars, and it is just the beginning of the play with sound and space in this piece (Example 3.2).

As the piece progresses, Beethoven heightens the aural complexity by means of hypermeter. Ordinarily, meter helps the synthesis and parsing of melody and phrase by highlighting a clear, regular downbeat. Here the regularity

EXAMPLE 3.2   Beethoven, String Quartet in C-sharp minor, No. 5, Presto, bars 20–36. Copyright G. Henle Verlag, Munich. Used with permission.

is suspended, or rather shifted. The effect is to keep the listener guessing as to where and how the phrase will end, as if the phrasing of the piece is in continual process of construction and deconstruction. The deconstruction is at its most bewildering in the pizzicato passages in bars 161–7, in which the sharing of the melody is taken to a limit, split note-wise between the instruments (Example 3.3). The construction becomes most emphatic at the end: the unison begins "sul ponticello" in bar 470, with "ordinario" bowing resuming at the crescendo in bar 487 (the passage described by the Prazák's viola player); this means that the full sound of the ensemble emerges gradually. Beethoven would have known that playing near the bridge emphasizes the upper harmonics at the expense of the fundamental pitch, producing a rather disembodied sound, which then becomes grounded at the conclusion, with a crescendo and resounding triple stops.

In a review of Op. 131 in 1828, Seyfried observes: "To give specific details of this quartet, without the comparative insight of the score, simply remains a problematic task."[39] Looking at the score can help determine how the

EXAMPLE 3.3   Beethoven, String Quartet in C-sharp minor, No. 5, Presto, bars 161–8. Copyright G. Henle Verlag, Munich. Used with permission.

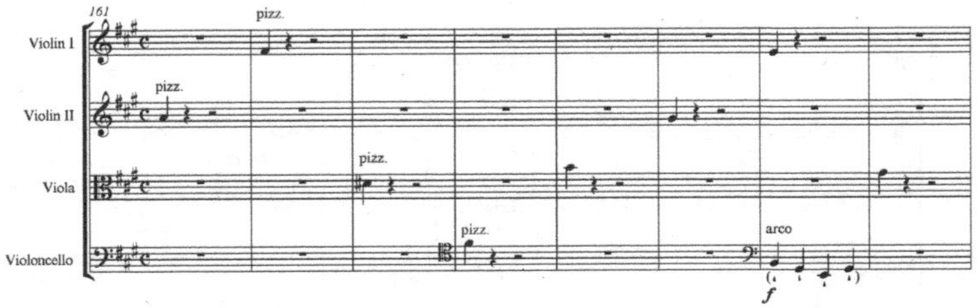

music is constructed—where a melody begins and ends and how the parts cohere. The Fry Street Quartet's first violinist even calls the score a "fifth voice" in rehearsal, and suggests rehearsing from the score to "create a more unified concept."[40] Early reviewers of Op. 131 noted the benefits of scores for performers (see Chapter 2). In other words, Beethoven's "new kind of part writing" places extreme demands on all of its listeners, including the performers; the kind of listening it calls for is greatly facilitated, as Rochlitz also found, by looking at all the parts together, that is, by visual cognition using scores.

Other contemporary commentators reached for visual and verbal aids. Score excerpts were used more often to illuminate their reviews and analyses of the work, such as in Helm's extensively illustrated discussion of Op. 131. The sheer amount written about the work suggests a constant striving to explicate it, to make it comprehensible for the listener. But in resorting to musical examples, visual metaphors, or (later on) analytical exegesis, scholars and critics were arguably steering the listener away from the work's purpose—and helping them to lose the point rather than find the essence. One early reviewer of Op. 133 complained of too much complexity, attributing this to the deafness: "Perhaps so much would not have been written down [i.e., in the score] if the master were also able to hear his own creations."[41] But in a deep, multivalent sense Beethoven was very well able to hear; so well as to enable a new kind of musical creation in the late quartets. On the other hand, many of his listeners—including the critic in question—could not or would not listen.

By deflecting attention onto the score and seeking to isolate abstract attributes such as "unity," construction, and resolution, we can miss the opportunity to engage in the work as an unfolding process and develop holistic hearing. Beethoven was arguably composing works as performances, using an embodied process that engaged sight and touch. The published score was a new phenomenon, often issued well after the original performance parts. Yes, he was keen to see scores of his works published, and would certainly have seen them as an aid to performance and understanding; but the idea that the work essentially resided in the score would have been foreign to him, even as music writers of his age, like Rochlitz, were starting to promote such an understanding of the musical work. Marx, one of the most influential critics and pedagogues of the time, did not. He actually devotes most of his review of scores of the late quartets to discussing performers and performance. As for listening, he clearly thought that it was a multivalent and individual phenomenon: the ability to "see" the often esoteric images suggested by music was the mark of a sophisticated listener.[42]

VIEWING AND FEELING VARIATIONS

By 1826 it had become very common to split themes between the parts in a string quartet. Beethoven had used this device to great effect in the first movement of the "Harp" quartet, where an arpeggio filters up through the parts and serves as a point of structural articulation in the exposition and at the point of recapitulation. The prominence of this device there, and his use of it in conjunction with pizzicato, must have helped to secure the quartet's nickname (created by his publisher). But the extent to which Beethoven uses and develops this device in Op. 131 is unprecedented. Melodic sharing is prominent in the opening fugue, where the voices are more or less "equal" in terms of their presentation of melodic material. But splitting themes and ideas is taken up much more variously in later movements; such sharing and splitting results in the quartet functioning as "one" instrument. The sense of the quartet functioning as one is also heightened in unison writing, found especially in movements two, five, and seven; and we have seen that extended sharing of an idea is especially prominent in No. 3 (here recitative).

Many writers are fixed on the finale as a culmination, and speak about the "finale problem."[43] But the sketches and the autograph show that, if Beethoven was working out any one big compositional "problem" in this quartet, it was a part-writing problem, and the effort was focused at the quartet's center, in the variations movement. At the core of the part writing, Beethoven develops the possibilities of sharing fragments of a theme between the voices, with multiple permutations. No. 4 contains seven sections, all quite different. Intensive work on part writing is most appreciable in the central (fourth) variation, where we see that even in the final writing out in the autograph, Beethoven was still grappling with the part sharing.

A theme and variations movement is an ideal place to develop and elaborate part writing. On its first presentation, No. 4's theme already represents considerable experimentation with sonority. Superficially at least, the first thirty-two bars of are in binary form: AA'BB'. But each phrase represents developments of the theme-splitting and sharing that is central to this quartet. During the first

A phrase, first and second violins share the theme; this is then reversed in A′, where the effect of splitting the theme is heightened by dissociating exchanges involving a series of three-octave leaps. The shifting timbres in the violins are emphasized still further, and made still more complex, by the divergent articulation of the two lower voices: sustained lines in the viola versus pizzicato in the cello. The variation has already begun.

Winter finds that it is "almost as if the unadorned statement [of the theme] had been omitted."[44] It can be argued that the "theme" here is not so much the melody as the idea of *sharing and splitting* the melody. The variations in these initial thirty-two bars involve both voice-leading and sonority. The effect, says Winter, is to "transform the repetitions of the A and B phrases into playgrounds for polyphonic manipulation."[45] The working out of the movement on these two axes cost Beethoven a great deal of work: numerous sketches and drafts, with re-working extending to the removal of several autograph leaves. They show him exploring the theme from many angles by way of melodic or motivic sharing and recombination of timbre.

Paging through the autograph manuscript reveals that it is largely free of alteration. Most of Beethoven's work toward the final version was carried out on the many sketch leaves. But not all of it. The autograph itself is divided between two libraries today. The Staatsbibliothek zu Berlin has the definitive version of Nos. 3 and 4; the Jagiellonian Library in Kraków has the complete autograph manuscript, in which these two movements appear as working drafts. In these drafts is extensive re-working of the substance in variation No. 4, especially from page 59, mid-way through the fourth variation. One part shows an unusual amount of revision: on p. 60, Beethoven even uses the lower staves of the page to squeeze in additional sketches (Figure 3.1). This work corresponds to bar 150 of the fourth movement, before the Allegretto and in the midst of a part that involves intensive voice-sharing of melodic ideas, and part pairing.

The changes that Beethoven made show him striving to preserve a sense of registral space between first violin and cello here. He was mainly working with the arpeggios in contrary motion, which provide the main action in the first half of the B and B′ phrases in variation 2. As Winter notes,

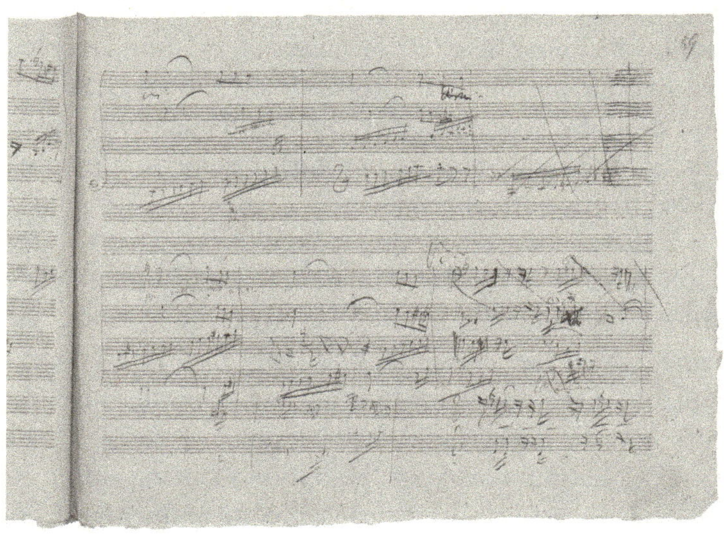

FIGURE 3.1   Autograph manuscript working draft of Beethoven's String Quartet in C-sharp minor, Op. 131, No. 4, page 60; showing far-reaching re-working of the substance in the fourth variation. (Courtesy of the Jagiellonian Library, Kraków.)

he was trying to preserve the opening up of space and the exhilarating effect of these cascading figures in the repeat as well, but could not do so by means of simple repetition of the two outer voices. Winter also observes that Beethoven is often working to preserve symmetry and thematic logic in sketches and drafts for the late quartets, going to great lengths to achieve structural cogency: "If we have long been aware of the special voice-leading qualities of the late quartets—buttressed by Beethoven's own remarks—the sketches for the variations provide a classic example of the lengths to which he was willing to go to honor these increased commitments."[46] Glauert seems to miss the point in speaking of this movement's "realization of a norm" and "impregnable solidity."[47] Although a sense of "flow" can certainly be found here (Helm speaks of an "uninterrupted flow like an ingenious improvisation"[48]), there is also a good deal of dissociating play, making the auditory space complex and rendering the movement more an unfolding process than a normalized form.

No survey of part-writing possibilities—which is arguably what this movement entails—would be complete without exploring the nature of quartet sound itself. The theme, which has been well and truly dissected and explored in terms of voice-leading and sonority, now recedes into the background. The background comes to the fore as Variation 5 explores the nature of string sound itself; while Variation 6 investigates accompanimental string textures. Most of variation 6 deploys *portato*, the typical mode of string accompaniment for a lyrical melody; but this variation differs from the typical pattern in that the lyrical melody is implied by the accompaniment, rather than supported by it. Ratner describes the end of variation five as "the most striking example of dealing with pure sounds" in Beethoven's quartet music.[49] Within a predominately legato articulation, Beethoven explores the sonorities most fundamental to the string quartet, perfect fifths, asking the players to perform numerous double stops. Some of these double stops could be fingered; but Beethoven's soft dynamic marking, together with "*dolce*," suggests that he expected them to be played using two open strings, a much more practical solution that allows the fundamental resonances of the string quartet instruments to ring out.

Thus Beethoven deploys visuality, physicality, and spatiality as compositional resources in Op. 131. The variations "dismember" and re-member the string quartet parts, examining their inner workings and recombining them. The listener who has the stamina to listen repeatedly and attentively gains a unique understanding of the genre in terms of both performance and composition. The experience for the performers too is unique, a test of stamina that can prove exhilarating. In a conversation book entry of 1826, Holz expressed alarm about the *attacca* performance of all seven movements: "Does it have to be played through without stopping? But then we won't be able to repeat anything! When are we supposed to tune?" An option mentioned in the conversation is to tune in the pause before the Presto; another was to perform it on a cool evening; and yet another was to buy reliable strings.[50] A more challenging option is to tune discreetly during the fifth variation, where Beethoven has written several opportunities into the score![51] Beethoven's new manner of part writing demands open-mindedness, lateral thinking, and agile responsiveness, on the part of performers and listeners alike.

CHAPTER 4

"LIKE AN OVERLY LARGE FANTASY"

THE IDEA OF FANTASY has been persistently and variously invoked regarding Op. 131, but never explored thoroughly. The idea of the free fantasia in Beethoven's day is itself slippery and has been used very diversely, raising the question of what fantasy clouds and/or illuminates. At one end of the interpretive spectrum, in 1828, Op. 131 struck Rochlitz as fecund and mercurial, "like an overly large fantasy," challenging the listener by "ever changing and transforming anew."[1] At the other, Leonard Ratner used the same metaphor in 1995, but to underscore the unity he found in Op. 131 as "a great single-movement composition, articulated along the lines of a fantasia." He does not find the work overly large or unduly variable; it fits into "the great plan of unity" whereby "Beethoven's compositional

Beethoven's String Quartet in C-sharp Minor, Op. 131. Nancy November, Oxford University Press.
© Oxford University Press 2021. DOI: 10.1093/oso/9780190059200.003.0005

strategies *connect, unify and give profile to* the form of this quartet."[2] Ratner argues that the entire quartet progresses in accentuation and articulation, from weak to strong, and from light to heavy. Like many other twentieth-century writers, he describes the finale as a culmination. A melodic thread is woven prominently through the work in the form of a "Pathetic figure"—the tetrachord motif heard in the opening fugue. He hears this figure returning in its original form in the finale to give "a final assertion of melodic unity to the quartet."[3] Ratner follows d'Indy in finding a "grand harmonic plan" in Op. 131: a work-level cadential formula that provides a larger unity than the local links between movements.

One can usefully compare Op. 131 to other fantasias, especially those of Beethoven, to canvass ways in which it is a fantasia, even if not so labeled, and to consider what this might have meant, and might mean now, in terms of listening experiences. This idea of a harmonic ground plan resembles C. P. E. Bach's conception of the free fantasia, and connects Op. 131 to various conceptions of the fantasia in the late eighteenth and early nineteenth centuries. But Ratner's perception of a readily apparent higher-level tonal or thematic unity in Op. 131 is contrary to the idea of the free fantasia in Beethoven's day, and suggests a quite different listening experience from the one reported by Rochlitz.

A more historically-grounded conception of Op. 131 as a fantasia is described briefly by Barbara Barry (2017), who asks us to consider parallels between Op. 131 and Beethoven's other important work in C-sharp minor, Op. 27, No. 2 (explicitly "Quasi una fantasia"). Both open with a slow movement, in a position virtually unprecedented in

Beethoven's works, with a meditative character, piano dynamics, and legato articulation; both end with finales propelled by intense rhythm (not so unusual for Beethoven). Barry argues: "While the substructure underpinning of the first movement is fugue, its expressive character, and perhaps even the work as a whole, as Ratner has suggested, is a fantasia."[4] In her argument "fantasia" becomes a musical "topic," that is, music in a style involving free development to be contrasted with the strictness of fugue.[5] But fantasia is more than a mere "topic" (one of a range of conventional subjects in musical composition in this era) in this work: it is a principal aesthetic idea.

STÜCKE

Stück has strong connotations in the context of nineteenth-century Romanticism, and specifically the fantasia. Tellingly, Beethoven preferred the word "Stück" (piece) rather than "movement" for each of the seven sections of Op. 131, which implies they are self-contained in some degree; they are distinct and complete in motivic substance, but without a formal rounding off.[6] Composers and authors of the era used the word *Stücke* to refer to individual pieces, each with a distinctive character, which could be assembled to form a collection to be heard or read together. *Stücke* were assembled at least as much for variety as for their conformation to an overarching theme. For example, the *Fantasiestücke in Callot's Manier* of E. T. A. Hoffmann (1814) brings together diverse stories in various genres—caricatures, a nocturne, satires, a fairy tale, critical pieces—under the rubric of "diary pages" from the travels of an "enthusiast." (The loosely autobiographical diary pages tell of a struggling composer with a history of misadventure in his bureaucratic career.) Modeled on the several series of etchings published by the fifteenth-century artist Jacques Callot, each piece is detailed and rich in its own right, bringing in self-reflection, irony, and humor (see Figure 4.1). The detail and precision of Callot's work was prized by contemporaries like Schumann, whose eight-part *Fantasiestücke*, Op. 12 (1837), was inspired by Hoffmann's *Fantasiestücke in Callot's Manier.*

The assembling of *Stücke* into collections did not imply that each individual piece was somehow deficient. Rather, each piece was self-contained, and even though there might be commonalities, it was the diversity of the individual pieces that recommended them for inclusion, and thus ultimately bound them together. This paradoxical conception has a philosophical underpinning in the late work of Beethoven's contemporary Friedrich Schlegel (1772–1829), who outlined a system embracing multiplicity, totality, and unity. Moving away from an earlier concern with organic unity, Schlegel speaks metaphorically of a "chemical system," which entails a merging ("Verschmelzung") of disparate elements. He applied this to his own literary fragments, which appeared in his literary magazine, *Athenaeum*; they were brief, pithy (almost prickly) statements, each exhibiting internal unity ("A fragment, like a small work of art, has to be entirely isolated from the surrounding world and be complete in itself like a hedgehog," *Athenaeumsfragment* 206).

The "unity" of each individual fragment reflects Schlegel's view that things do not come together as a finalized totality

FIGURE 4.1   Jacques Callot (1592–1635); "Masked Dwarf with Contorted Legs" and "Dwarf with Violin" (from a series of 21 etchings, *Varie Figure Gobbi*, 1616). (Courtesy of Alamy images.)

but exist in a "chaotic universality" of infinitely opposing forces and positions.[7] Something like a critical mass—a plenitude of fragments—would, however, exert a kind of force field of reciprocal pressures and attractions. Such a force field thrives on difference and incoherence. It does not rely on the teleology of dialectics suggested by Barry's understanding of Op. 131. For Barry the opening slow first movement fugue, leading to a rhythmically charged tonic minor finale, describes an overall trajectory from reflection to resolution, and from contemplation to defiance.[8] Nor does Schlegel's conception entail any kind of "organic" developmental narrative (such as Ratner's). He envisions a series of oscillations between "part" and "whole." "Wholeness" in this system is less a state of being than of becoming, as reflected in Schlegel's verbs—*werden, enstehen, verschmelzen*: to become, to develop, to merge.[9]

Beethoven's specific development of this idea of oscillation is most clearly illustrated by the transitions between sections in Op. 131: here attractive and repulsive, centripetal and centrifugal forces can be observed at work. The fugue (labeled "No. 1" by Beethoven) proceeds to No. 2 by means of the octave leap and the fermata on the raised seventh of the new key (D major). Only the momentary silence and surprising semitone shift via pivot note holds up the flow. The transition to No. 3 is a more striking call to attention: soft chords, spaced by silence, sound the tonic and third of the D major chord. To this dyad, the third is added below, producing the tonic of B minor at the opening of No. 3, which opens with two Striking chords (tonic–V^6), again spaced by silence. A major in No. 4 is prepared by what would have been a conventional cadence in E major at the end of No. 3 (that is, the dominant of the new key); but this is derailed at the last minute by D naturals in the penultimate chord. No. 4 ends, for a change, on the tonic; but again the cadence is destabilized by the lowered sixth and seventh scale degrees in the preceding bar; and the two final tonic chords are sounded on weak beats, *piano*, pizzicato, and incorporate octave leaps, foreshadowing the rhythmic play to come. The most abrupt connection yet is between Nos. 5 and 6: No. 5 ends with an octave leap incorporating the tonic chord, followed by a shift up a major third for an octave leap on the new tonic, G sharp. And the link to No. 7 is even more startlingly direct: No. 6 simply cadences into it, introducing the B-sharp raised-seventh of the "home tonic" at the last moment (Example 4.1). Transitions, in Op. 131, become ever more concise and pithy.

Pronounced articulation between movements was usual at this time in traditional instrumental genres—sonata, quartet, symphony. Op. 131 resists this with a smoothing over of joinery—so as to create one long form, especially as the transitions foreshadow gestures from the ensuing movements. But locally these transitions often heighten a sharp change of affect from one section to the next: the effects of oblique tonal shifts and unexpected silences are at least as destabilizing as they are smoothing. The transitions between the adjacent variations of No. 4 show the same simultaneous concern with smoothing and articulation, neither one necessarily dominating. On the one hand, textures flow more or less seamlessly from one variation to the next, with some help from subtle and varied linking devices such as the passing of a figure down through the voices, or first violin solo. On the other hand each variation is set off by a different treatment of the downbeat at its beginning,

EXAMPLE 4.1   Beethoven, String Quartet in C-sharp minor: (a) transition from No. 5 (from bar 489) to No. 6 (bars 1–4); (b) transition from No. 6 (from bar 24) to No. 7 (bars 1–5). Copyright G. Henle Verlag, Munich. Used with permission.

(a)
489
Violin I
Violin II
Viola
Violoncello
(cresc.)
f
496
Vln. I
Vln. II
Vla.
Vc.
(ff)
No. 6 Adagio quasi un poco andante
p
cresc.
p mezza voce
attacca
(b)
24
Violin I
Violin II
Viola
Violoncello
sf
dim.
p
cresc.
p
No. 7
1
Allegro
Vln. I
Vln. II
Vla.
Vc.
ff
(i)

which is subtly destabilizing. The theme begins, as it were, one quaver beat "late"; variation 1 begins one quaver beat "early"; variations 2, 4, and 5 begin on the downbeat, variation 4 being further marked by an *sfp* accent in all voices; and variations 3 and 6 are one crotchet beat "late" (Example 4.2). Transitions are marked in this work, drawing the

EXAMPLE 4.2   The connections and disconnections between variations in No. 4 from Op. 131: (a) theme, bars 1–4; (b) variation 1, bars 32–36; (c) variation 6, bars 187–90; showing the theme beginning, respectively, "early," on the downbeat and "late." Copyright G. Henle Verlag, Munich. Used with permission.

listener's attention to the act of transitioning—more often perceived as a subordinate process by definition.

Beethoven's *Stücke* concept, of distinctive pieces set together in an evocative open-ended chaos, aligns with Schlegel's view that the Romantic artwork is in a constant state of becoming, never reaching perfection of form; or rather, questing for a sublimity that would always be just beyond reach. The Romantic ideal tends to render the idea of distinct genres (of poetry, in the first instance) meaningless. However, Schlegel proposes that the Romantic artwork ideal—which he generalizes as a single "infinite book," a new Bible—will eventually replace the fragmentary aspirations of distinct genres with a higher unity than that of Classical poetry. At this end point, all the separate genres—which in their Classical understanding (as epic, lyric, and dramatic poetry) were "ridiculous in their strict purity"—will be reunited. Until then, we are left with a confusion of genres.[10] Roger Ferris argues that Schumann's view of the musical artwork can be paralleled with Schlegel's: Schumann lamented the state of confusion he found over musical genres, in which Classical genres based on the sonata cycle had apparently run their course but no large-scale replacement had emerged.[11] But he found value in the resulting originality, and the potential for self-realization and growth in the small ("lesser") genres so popular in his day.[12] Beethoven was just as explicitly concerned with manipulating generic boundaries.

Beethoven's late quartets, which combine miniatures with movements of great length, each with a premium on originality, seem to undergo a comparable ideational development to that seen in the work of Schegel and Schumann. The concatenation of *Stücke* in the late quartets reaches ever further, Op. 132, 130, and 131 having respectively five, six, and seven "movements." These three works are also linked by tonality (A minor, B-flat major, C-sharp minor) and are thematically linked in their references to the four notes of the second tetrachord of the harmonic minor scale. In these ways, they form a kind of "meta opus" with a linking motivic thread, but each so radically different that this commonality is seldom noted in the literature.[13] Op. 131 demonstrates acute concern with the larger idea and aesthetics of *Stücke*—a concern with beginnings, endings, and transitions.

FANTASY

Schlegel's understanding of the Romantic artwork was so broad that it called into question not only the idea of discrete genres, but even of distinct arts. Ultimately, all the separate poetic genres would be reunited at the end of literature, poetry merging with philosophy and rhetoric.[14] The idea was to bring together music, pictorial arts, and literature in a kind of universal, multivalent artwork: in Schlegel's account the Romantic artwork implied and sought a synesthetic merging. In this context the fantasia came into its own, reaching toward the Romantic ideal. For instance, literary fantasies of the nineteenth century are multivalent in ambition, operating textually, visually, and psychologically. Hoffmann, for example, aspired not only to evoke figures in the eyes of the reader, but, through his narrative technique, to express the "brilliance of color in the inner eye," to invoke a multi-sensory experience in an ostensibly mono-sensory genre.[15]

In Beethoven's Op. 131 the plurality of musical materials invites and demands multivalent reception, as did other nineteenth-century fantasias (see also Chapter 3). On one level, the quartet is full of different kinds of music—many sub-genres, lyric (one thinks, for example, of the lilting melody pervading No. 2), dramatic (the recitative that is No. 3) and epic (No. 1, the lengthy and striking opening fugue). It is as if the composer wanted to prove that there was no one right mode of expression in string quartet writing; or, like Schumann and Schlegel, to celebrate the possibilities for expansion and self-actualization offered by the concatenation of small forms—here fugue, dance, recitative, theme and variations, and so forth. The work is especially groundbreaking in the way it combines diverse genres to arrive at a completely new concept of string quartet form. Diverse music per se is just one of its modes. Beethoven does not just compose music from multiple available kinds of music and ways of sounding that music. He also explores, and invites the listener to explore, sonority and sonic invention itself.

Open-ended and investigative, fantasia might seem to be quite the opposite of the formalized string quartet genre as it was starting to be understood by Beethoven's time. Fantasia in string quartets was not entirely new. It had appeared before, as a topic or a movement. Chamber music lovers in early nineteenth-century Vienna would have been familiar with instances by Haydn and Beethoven. Earlier string quartets with a substantial fantasia component include Haydn's Op. 20, No. 2 (the second movement is labeled "Capricco"); the "gypsy violin"-like and tonally wide-ranging slow movement of Op. 54; and Op. 76, No. 6

(its slow movement is labeled "Fantasia"). Beethoven had also incorporated fantasia elements into his later string quartets, without labeling them as such, attracting some adverse reactions. A reviewer of Op. 74 in 1811 referred to "free fantasia" in connection with the work's diverse affects. The review depicted the work as problematically diverse, an inward seriousness in the first movement being disturbed by whimsical pizzicato and a "savage national war dance" in the third; the unruly work fell short of expectations for the string quartet and had "more the appearance of a free fantasia than of a well-governed whole." The second half of the adagio strayed close to the very limits of fine art, the reviewer found.[16]

Despite these precedents, and some not always well-received surprises from Beethoven such as the Grosse Fuge, listeners and performers in 1820s Europe had no reason to expect a string quartet that was itself a large-scale fantasia. The two concepts were almost diametrically opposed in contemporary theory, even though Beethoven's quartets from the middle period onwards had been challenging people's expectations. Audiences would have expected a Beethoven string quartet to be a weighty, four-movement work with an emphasis on a sonata form, *thematische Arbeit* (motivic working) between parts, and an overall tonal plan based on one or two primary key areas.[17] Since the late eighteenth century the string quartet had been the most privileged form of chamber music, the touchstone of compositional skill, to which only the most accomplished composer could aspire. Unity was highly prized in the "true" string quartet—the "well-governed whole" that the reviewer quoted above finds Op. 74 wanting. Petiscus went so far as to describe the string quartet as "a [holy] *four-fold unification*, in which the unity of the whole and the individuality of each of the four voices mutually circumscribe each other."[18] Unity in this sense was partly about the way the work should sound in performance, but above all about tonal and thematic coherence.

"Fantasia," on the other hand, denotes not only a genre, but also, as Annette Richards has it, "a musical aesthetic that enters into, destabilizes, and complexifies other genres of instrumental music."[19] The fantasia was set in opposition to standard instrumental genres, and perhaps especially opposed to the ideal string quartet, at the fundamental level—the level of ontology or "work concept." Whereas the string quartet (and other instrumental genres) should properly stay within the formal and compositionally conceived limits of the fine arts (in this instance, three or four distinctive movements; an emphasis on sonata forms), the fantasia was open-ended as to which musical materials were admitted and particularly how they were developed.[20] Richards describes fantasia as an "anti-genre," in that it has no fixed expectations for the composer or listener to play with or against.[21] It was understood as expressing something like a stream of consciousness, so that the composer's *Erfinding* (process of invention) is based on his mood. Christian Friedrich Michaelis explained this conception in his 1805 essay on humor in music for the *Allgemeine musikalische Zeitung*, where he discusses the free fantasia (or capriccio):

[In the capriccio] the composer seems to be too dependent on his immediate mood and upon ideas that are generated by it to have in mind an audience or to attempt to entertain it and engage its sympathy by means of comprehensible ideas. He seems rather to be impelled by an inner urge to lay bare his immediate soul and to express the strange succession and transformation of emotions and ideas to which he is subject.[22]

When unity comes up in early nineteenth-century discourse about fantasia, it often refers to the listener's perception of a (unified) human subject or persona in the work, such as Michaelis's compositional persona whose soul is "laid bare" for us. So Beethoven's Op. 27, No. 2 attracts special praise: "This fantasy is from beginning to end a solid whole, originating all at once from the entire, profound and fervently agitated soul, as if hewn from a single block of marble."[23]

In the environment in which Beethoven's late quartets emerged, fantasia can be understood as a manner of musical unfolding that transcends the materiality of text and performance, but is circumscribed by the feelings and ideas of the composer, and finally coheres within the listener's understanding of the work. This contrasts with the emphasis on compositional unity made by Ratner and many other scholars of the twentieth and twenty-first centuries, but it resonates with Wagner's earlier idea of Op. 131 as "a day in the life of our Saint," if not with his narrow idea of how it should be listened to; and strikingly with Lenz's description of the work as consisting of "stories of great souls."[24] Helm comes closest to Michealis with his more extended account of Op. 131's musical persona, even if he ultimately seeks out unity in terms of musical themes (see Chapter 1):

The implementation of a certain psychological idea is unmistakable [in Op. 131], as in a few string quartets. It is none other than the elevation of the severely tested noble man's soul from the darkest night of the deepest melancholy to a liberating humor, to victory over the overpowering energy of fate's hostile demons, to inner reconciliation.[25]

Reviewers in Beethoven's day differed on this kind of unity, which resided suspiciously in the affective realm and called for a demanding kind of listening. When it was appropriately labeled, and performed in the right setting in the expected medium—especially packaged and received as virtuosic or sentimental keyboard music—the free fantasia was accepted and praised. So, for example, an 1813 reviewer who complained that composers had recently ignored the free fantasia applauded Beethoven's keyboard Fantasia in G minor, Op. 77, as an exception, a remnant of "true" fantasy in the style of C. P. E. Bach. But, said the more conservative critics, fantasia encroached on other genres and threatened to erode hallowed cultural spaces. A critic in 1817 complained of the infiltration of fantasia into just about every genre of the day:

It appears to me as if the fantasy, like a despot, has seized absolute power over music . . . One can no longer perceive either any definite musical forms or any limits to the influence of the fantasy. Everything goes in all directions but to no fixed destination; the madder the better! The wilder and stranger, all the more novel and effective. In such a way we hear and play nothing but fantasies. Our sonatas are fantasies, our overtures are fantasies and even our symphonies, at least those of Beethoven and his like, are fantasies.[26]

Fantasia seemed to be taking over—happily for those who, like Schumann, would celebrate it as progress toward the ideal Romantic artwork. For conservative critics, though, it was shocking, most shocking when it intruded on canonic genres like the symphony. A German philosopher, Amadeus Wendt, spoke of Beethoven's "gross Errors": the composer was creating his own romantic musical work in which fantasy rules—to the detriment of proper harmonic coherence and the structured connection of ideas.[27] Wendt was the first to use the term "Classical Period" to embrace Haydn, Mozart, and Beethoven, giving rise to the concept of Viennese Classicism in music. Beethoven's excursions into fantasia were a counter-example that threatened to disrupt this tidy historiographical plan, especially for those who placed the symphonies and string quartets of Beethoven among the principal cultural products of Viennese classicism.[28]

FANTASIA, OP. 131, AND THE LISTENER

Proponents of the free fantasia argued that it was, par excellence, a work for the connoisseur listener, who would understand listening not as teleological (purposive and goal-directed) but rather as phenomenological (entailing personal experience and process). On this level we can see many connections with Beethoven's late quartets, especially Op. 131. Listening to fantasias was only for the initiate prepared to journey through complex sonic labyrinths. As Richards notes, critics from the first decades of the nineteenth century in the *Allgemeine musicalische Zeitung* extolled fantasias that allowed imaginative scope while maintaining a "tight hidden thread" that "runs through the whole and can be perceived, if not by the fleeting beholder, by an experienced lover of art." Made properly, the fantasia's "subtle connections" would appeal to superior players and listeners, those with "the intellect and inclination for the deeper art." Such connections were "the more to be praised the more cleverly they are hidden" and the juxtaposition of affects "neither too precipitous, whereby the sections would appear too fragmentary, nor too tame, whereby the whole would become more like a sonata."[29] Fantasias were difficult and exceptional, then; their "inner essence" was to be discovered (if at all) only from the fantasias of C. P. E. Bach.

Bach was a touchstone not only because of his numerous keyboard rondos and fantasias, but also because of his theory of the free fantasia, which he partially disclosed in the second book of his *Versuch uber die wahre Art das Clavier zu spielen* (1762). Bach explained in this influential treatise that there is method in the apparent madness of the free fantasia, especially as regards harmonic links.[30] The free fantasia is in some respects an elaborate realization of a figured bass (see Figure 4.2). It is based on a harmonic plan, which might be seen as a very extended cadence with many harmonic twists along the way. Third relations, enharmonic shifts, and pivot chords and notes are all fair game. But these shifts, however oblique, must always be in some way logical. Here Beethoven's tonal overviews come to mind. He started to develop them in connection with Op. 131 in particular, and they seem to point to the large-scale cadence as the underlying structural template for Op. 131 as a whole.[31] They certainly suggest some planning at movement level and work level.

FIGURE 4.2   "Von der Freyen Fantasie," C. P. E. Bach, *Versuch über die wahre Art das Clavier zu spielen*, 1762 (Berlin), pp. 341ff., showing the harmonic ground plan in the form of a figured bass and its realization (at least in notation) as free fantasia.

But for the fantasia as a listening experience, rather than a compositional process, a *sense of lost direction* was called for, of being immersed in a structure whose shape is unclear, even undiscoverable. So in the discourse about musical fantasias, labyrinths and untamed, wild, or "English" gardens are used as metaphors for the listening experience.[32] The fantasia character of Op. 131, in this connection, derives especially from the local destabilization in the various transitions between the sections, with their oblique tonal shifts of the kind used by Bach. Rochlitz's metaphor of a goldminer's exploration is an apt expansion of the landscape gardening metaphor of fantasia discourse into uncultivated lands, suggesting the various, vast, and sometimes intimidating auditory terrain of Op. 131.

The C-sharp minor quartet can be compared to other fantasias and other fantasia-like works by Beethoven in terms of their procedures and their effects on the listener. Above all, these works exhibit a strong sense of unfolding process, without many traditional formal signposts, which means that to follow them the listener must engage intently with them, listening (and generally sensing) moment-by-moment. In particular, fantasias often conveyed an impression of spontaneous utterance, of meaning being put together on the spot, as Kleist advocated in his *Über die allmähliche Verfertigung der Gedanken beim Reden* (*About the Gradual Production of Thoughts in Speaking*, 1805).[33] "Utterance" is especially pertinent to the cadenzas and recitatives of Nos. 3 and 4, which invoke spontaneous vocal declamation. But there are strategically placed, unexpected silences, too, for example after the structural dominant in No. 3 or at moments of expected thematic return in No. 5.

They force us to wait, and listen. Expected visual signposts are also absent; for example the double barlines, in whose place we find single barlines (Figure 4.3).[34] Single barlines are undermined in the hypermeter of No. 5. In these ways, Op. 131, like other fantasias of the era, sits somewhere between improvisation and composition, pushing away the constraints of musical notation, eluding conformity to musical form, and depending for their meaning and understanding on performance.

FIGURE 4.3   Autograph manuscript of Op. 131 showing the transition from No. 3 to No. 4 on one and the same page and with a single bar line. (Courtesy of the Staatsbibliothek zu Berlin—Preußischer Kulturbesitz; Musikabteilung mit Mendelssohn-Archiv. Mus. ms.autogr. Beethoven, L. v., Mendelssohn-Stiftung 19, p. 2.)

Fantasias demanded attentive listening in order to follow their various and complex unfolding forms. But this does not mean that the listener becomes sutured into the work by its immediacy—as the reader of sentimental and epistolary novels of the time was supposed to be, for example. Rather, like certain other narrative types of the era, fantasias were expected to engender a self-conscious listening practice involving the alternation of passionate sentiment and ironic critique. It is not unusual to find in fantasias a *lieto fine* finale, which sits in contrast to earlier more melancholy movements and renders them ironic with a kind of "annihilating humor" in the manner of Jean Paul, to whom Beethoven was compared.[35] Helm suggests alternatively that the second movement can already be heard as a kind of "liberating humor," an antidote to the musical persona's melancholy musings—circular, sustained, studied—in No. 1.[36] No. 2 starts circular and sustained, but quickly brushes this model to the side, without completely abandoning it. A similar process unfolds in Bach's Fantasia in F-sharp minor, H. 536 (*C. P. E. Bachs Empfindungen*), which starts with a halting, deeply felt slow movement and ends with a rollicking rondo, "framing private sorrow as an aesthetic experience, distanced and commodified."[37] Beethoven's Sonata in E-flat major, Op. 27, No. 1, which has *attacca* indications between the movements typical for fantasias of the time, also ends with a *lieto fine*.[38]

Beethoven's Sonata in A major, Op. 101 has quite a few similarities to Op. 131 in its process: it opens *in medias res* with the performance inscription "Etwas lebhaft und mit der innigsten Empfindung" (somewhat lively with the deepest feeling). But this statement of feeling is immediately disputed by the much more lively, dotted F major second movement. Rather than making a clear opening statement, Op. 131 likewise emerges as if in mid-thought, the first four notes in the solo violin forming something like a heavy sigh; and the ensuing fugue could be taken to represent deep and difficult feelings. Helm's calling No. 1 the "darkest night of the deepest melancholy" can be understood in terms of the fugal technique, which at the time was associated with erudition and study, both linked historically to melancholy. No. 2 is similarly light-hearted; and the finale, like that in Op. 101, is *attacca,* and contrasts sharply with the prayerful and deeply felt No. 6 finale, with, at the very last moment, a high-spirited turn to the major. These affective juxtapositions jolt the listener out of any complacency and inspire active engagement with the work; but, as critics had it, only by listeners who had the "intellect and inclination for the deeper art."

Attentive listening is also implied by the fantasia offering itself to multiple readings. On the formal level, the listener can decide which kind of form might be unfolding, in the subtle play against more formal genres like the sonata and rondo. On the affective level, the listener might be held in suspense by what the musical persona will do next. In the case of Op. 131, we might ask: is the melancholic of No. 1 ever going to triumph, especially after the radical flat-side plunge and persistent circularity of theme and harmony in No. 2? Formally, the answer is unclear: is No. 2 a sonata or a rondo, both, or neither? Among the many analysts who place this movement "in" a particular form, there is a consensus that it is a sonata form without a development. But Friedhelm Krummacher, for instance, says it is a clear rondo.[39] Indorf finds that the decision as to form depends on the listener: it only matters for analysis if a sonata form without a development *sounds* different to a rondo.[40] At first No. 2 seems to offer the listener a dance theme. But rondo form seems less and less likely the longer one listens, as a growing complexity tends to belie the opening. But nor is it a clear-cut sonata form, since it does not have the thematic development or "development section" required. So, in affective terms, the persona never actually achieves the liberation that the apparently sanguine theme promises.

MELANCHOLIA, FANTASIA, AND THE MEANING OF TIME

Which way will the musical persona tend in Op. 131? Toward liberation, or toward destructive melancholia? Modern-day popular reception of the work favors the latter narrative (see Chapter 2), the idea that a dark strand of melancholia predominates in the work, leading to tragedy. For the nineteenth-century listener, part of the answer lay in the work's framing key: C-sharp minor, according to Christian Schubart's influential *Ideen zu einer Aesthetik der Tonkunst* (1806), signals "penitential lamentation" but also "intimate conversation with God, the friend and help-meet of life," so both "sighs of disappointed friendship and love lie in its radius."[41] A melancholic portrayed in C-sharp minor was thus not beyond help, and would incline more toward the creative fantasia described by Johann Georg Zimmermann than the degenerative melancholy and fantasia described by Immanuel Kant.[42] Kant describes the problematic fantasia in terms of deteriorating melancholia: "he hits upon the grotesque—meaningful dreams, presentiments, and miraculous portents. He is in danger of becoming a visionary [ein Phantast] or a crank."[43]

Zimmerman, to the contrary, asserts that lively imagination and fantasy can combat the adverse effects of melancholy.[44] A strengthening kind of melancholy is felt above all by the solitary wanderer. Recalling his own solitary rambles in an English garden, he observes that the beautiful unification of art and nature effected "an innocent fantasy in the heart."[45] Such solitude "transforms . . . deep sorrow into sweet melancholy" (verwandelt . . . tiefe Schwermuth in süsse Melankolie).[46] According to Zimmermann, melancholy can effect personal and thence social transformation. The key, he finds, is that it prompts self-reflection: "melancholy is the school of humility, and self-disdain is the first step toward self-knowledge."[47] In Op. 131, such transformations arguably take place principally in the A major variations, which, tonally speaking, sit half-way up from the initial flat-side plunge (to D major in No. 2), and the extremely sharp-side home tonic (reached again in the Finale). The variations themselves, explored in Chapter 3, suggest manifold, thoroughgoing reflection to the point of examining sonority itself—and in the key associated with hopeful expectation.[48]

But melancholia, like the fantasia, is not a tidy category, neither formally nor in terms of affect. In Dürer's seminal *Melencolia I* (Figure 4.4) the disorderly, abundant array of symbols lacks a formal center. Joseph Leo Koerner describes this work as purposefully obscure, demanding not only interpretive labor but reflection on the same: "The vast effort of subsequent interpreters, in all their industry

FIGURE 4.4   Albrecht Dürer, *Melencolia I* (1514), engraving, 31 × 26 cm.
(Courtesy of UCLA Grunwald Center for the Graphic Arts.)

and error, testifies to the efficacy of the print as an occasion for thought. Instead of mediating *a* meaning, *Melencolia* seems designed to generate multiple and contradictory readings."[49] Such an argument can also be made for Op.

131, which has proved to be one of Beethoven's most elusive works and has engendered a correspondingly substantial literature.

Since the fifteenth century, melancholia had been thought a paradoxical temperament that engendered both pleasure and pain; and it was persistently associated with disturbing reflections. The melancholic shows a particularly troubled relationship with time: the limits of earthly time versus limitless eternity are figured in works of art by such emblems as hourglasses, ruins, scales that evaluate, bells to toll time, and vanishing horizons, as in *Melencholia I*. These emblems still featured in images of Beethoven's day, by artists such as Francisco Goya and Caspar David Friedrich, who depict subjects similarly contemplating such topics as beauty, creativity, and mortality.

In musical representations of melancholy, including Beethoven's own, a troubled relationship with time can be represented by musical ideas that come back to haunt— ideas from the musical past like fugue and counterpoint, and ideas from earlier in the piece of music in question, like the tetrachord in the case of Op. 131. Melancholy is no new mood for Beethoven, but something he explored throughout his career. We see this in "La malinconia," the penultimate movement from his String Quartet Op. 18, No. 5. The ensuing Allegro might be heard as a resolution to the melancholy mood. The pulse is lively, the harmonic rhythm immediately clear; but two equally clear references back to the Adagio suggest that the depths of preceding depression cannot be fully erased from La Malinconia's memory.[50] Fantasias often contain passages of reminiscence toward their end, running counter to the affirmative closure demanded by the conventional drama of sonata form—or the overly jolly *lieto fine*. Op. 27, No. 1 inserts an Adagio fragment close to its end, producing "a curiously hasty, over-emphatic and unsatisfactory ending," according to Richards.[51] She finds Op. 101 "imbued with the fantastic confusion of past and present . . . the first movement theme 'haunts' the work."[52]

The same could be said of Op. 131, which begins with an emphatic evocation of the past, and, confusingly, starts where the traditional string quartet would rightly end, with a fugue. The finale then shows great reluctance to actually end. Not only does it refer us back to the beginning, with an oblique reference to the opening fugue, but it refuses to use this material to help effect closure. Quite the opposite: the fugal recall, should the savvy listener find this thread, suggests a continued preoccupation with the past that cannot be circumvented by conventional closure. In fact the recapitulation and coda compound the destabilizing effect of the fugal recall by denying the anticipated confirmation of the tonic: the recapitulation begins with a drastic swerve back to the flat side, to D major. A long chain of C-sharp minor cadences in the coda try to affirm the home tonic forcefully, rather than confirm it logically. A tonally wider-ranging coda with particular digressions to the sharp side might have helped restabilize; but this section does more to confirm the still-present flat-side with sub-dominant (F-sharp minor) chords. The final few seconds of wind-up tonic major chords do more to convey a "curiously hasty, over-emphatic, and unsatisfactory" end (in Richards's words) than to conclude the work in the expected way.

I disagree with Kinderman that the fugue has a strong presence in the finale, hearing it more as fleeting and elusive—a loose thread that threatens to take us back into the maze. But I concur with his hearing of the final parts of the work: "The denial and weakening of closure allows for a paradoxical continuity, a kind of continued life in the imagination of the work as a whole." So the quartet invites replaying in the mind's ear, but not so much as "an experience that transcends merely linear concepts of time and termination," as Kinderman hears it.[53] Rather it implies that the persona of the quartet—and we as listeners—might continue to reflect, contemplating, for instance, the contradiction between linear time and all eternity.

CHAPTER 5

OP. 131 AND THE RISE OF ATTENTIVE LISTENING

MODERN-DAY RECEPTION: PERFORMANCE AND COMPOSITION

We have seen how scholars, especially in the twentieth century, tend to dwell on the issue of unity, repeatedly setting out to show how Op. 131 is unified in compositional (thematic and tonal) terms. A similar tendency also often appears in recent popular reception (see Chapter 2). The concept of *Stücke* recognizes variation, but within a holistic unity of assembled pieces. But modern-day reception can also run in quite contrary directions. An example from the modern-day compositional reception of Op. 131 is Mark Andre's ensemble work *riss 2* (crack/rupture), which premiered in 2014 with Ensemble Modern conducted by Lukas Vis in the Frankfurt (Main) Alte Oper music festival

Beethoven's String Quartet in C-sharp Minor, Op. 131. Nancy November, Oxford University Press.
© Oxford University Press 2021. DOI: 10.1093/oso/9780190059200.003.0006

alongside Op. 131.[1] *riss 2* responds explicitly to Op. 131 on several levels that have nothing to do with compositional unity in any traditional sense; rather, *riss 2* emphasizes the act of transitioning, which is arguably central to Op. 131, and focuses on fissures between pieces rather than on their unity. Martin Zenck suggests that these two works can, in similar ways, disrupt our understanding of musical works in terms of structure, sound transformations, and especially sense of time.[2]

Andre's work, for a chamber group of sixteen performers, comprises fourteen miniatures. On a structural level an analogy with Op. 131's seven sections and seven variations might be inferred. In terms of sound transformations (discussed in Chapter 3), the fourth and fifth variations of Op. 131 No. 4 in particular explore the very fabric of quartet writing—the sounds and ways of sounding that are possible in the quartet. Andre and Beethoven also both investigate time by compositional means. Chapter 4 describes how Op. 131's fourteen sections are both articulated and connected by transitions; and how the work itself enacts transition, emerging on a sigh motif in the solo violin of the opening fugue, and in the Finale departing without a solid conclusion in the home tonic. The work invokes melancholy, via the recall of fugue as a music of the past, and the rehearing of No. 1's opening gesture in No. 7. These affective and compositional features all call attention to time and its passing.

riss 2 takes the exploration of sound and time much further. Its fourteen sections are all sonically explorative. *riss 2* requires, for example, the violin and viola players to bow on their bridges, the cellist on the tailpin, the percussionist on the edge of a cymbal. These techniques excite high-frequency partials—components of any pitch produced on an instrument that are usually considered secondary, but nonetheless contribute to defining timbre and its development in time. Wind players must overblow, again emphasizing transient or "inessential" components of pitch. The sounding parts of *riss 2* are thus largely made up of what might be considered marginal sounds. Meanwhile silence is woven into the composition in a way that demands attentive and patient reflective listening. As the final reverberations die away, for instance, all the players must sit poised in playing position so that the audience, too, remains poised and attentive (Figure 5.1). Thus the work develops an intense interest in interspaces, interims, and transitions at the local and the "work" level.

Both *riss 2* and Op. 131 might be understood as large-scale fantasias (see chapter 4), or variations, which invite reflection on the very idea of listening to chamber music, and promote attentive listening. In both works the experience

FIGURE 5.1   Players poised at the end of Mark Andre's *riss 2*, ensemble oktopus (2017).

of time is potentially different from what might be expected in the concert setting: the listener is not the passive recipient (more or less attentive) of a wash of enjoyable and edifying sounds, but ideally engages actively in a very challenging task, ultimately being asked to consider what "the work" actually consists of, in essence. In the case of Op. 131, can the slow fugue really be an opening movement? What is the form of No. 2? Is No. 3 actually a movement, or an eleven-bar transition? These are aspects that have puzzled those listeners who are theoretically knowledgeable about traditional forms; they will baffle all the more listeners who are less acquainted with European art music of this era. As we have seen, scholars from the late nineteenth-century onwards have answered these questions variously. With *riss 2*, the questions are much more pointed, but essentially similar: where does the work begin, if indeed it does begin? Are there any "movements" as such? Where does the work end? The critic who tries to answer such questions definitively can miss that the point of these works is provoking engaged listening. Both works can be taken less as products, with ultimately comprehensible forms, and more as processes, in which the listener continually tries to comprehend forms and follow fluctuating affects.

Richards says that when a fantasia is performed, "the ear is distracted from the underlying form by the disconcertingly fragmented surface."[3] This will happen inevitably with *riss 2*, with its extensive use of performance techniques to destabilize the work, drawing attention to transitions and transitioning. But distraction from the underlying form will not necessarily result when listening to a modern performance of Op. 131. Zenck finds that only a few performers realize Op. 131 with the necessary "centrifugal power," citing the Juilliard String Quartet from 1960.[4] The Juilliard's use of rubato and portato in this recording helps: both expressive devices (common in nineteenth-century performance) alert the listener to fine nuances and surface details, conveying a sense of spontaneous delivery if not downright fragmentation. Ultimately, however, recording technology tends to disallow the kind of immediacy that is needed. The recording takes in the Juilliard performance coincide with the boundaries of the work's *Stücke*; this disrupts the aesthetic idea, which depends on both centrifugal and centripetal forces, exerted especially at the transitions.

Other influences in the recording age tend to minimize the fragmentary surface character of the work: as a result of editing and the constant striving for ever more "perfect" performance, recordings of Op. 131 have taken on a certain polish and sameness of timbre. On the one hand Beethoven certainly intended the work for highly accomplished performers. Performing this work demands in particular an excellent sense of ensemble, as the modern-day string quartets quoted in Chapter 3 remarked. It is necessary in order to realize the sense of unified "utterance" in this quartet, something arguably much easier to do in a fantasia for piano solo, for instance. Bodily gestures and eye contact help, as can be seen in the lifting and breathing in the transition from Nos. 1–2 in a 2016 live performance of the Chamber Music Society at the Lincoln Centre.[5]

On the other hand, Beethoven would have chosen C-sharp minor as the home tonic of Op. 131 with particular affective intent: in this key few open strings are available to quartet players (especially in the opening fugue, with its use of E sharps), which reduces resonance and lends an elusive, otherworldly aura to Nos. 1 and 7. Applying vibrato throughout the work, and striving to approximate "pure" or just intonation, as many modern quartet ensembles do, undermines Beethoven's careful choice of keys and negates the disruptive centrifugal power. At the transition to No. 2, for example, D major will otherwise contrast markedly with the C minor fugue, being one of the most resonant keys for the violin, with all open strings available.[6] Quatuor Ébène's 2016 live performance demonstrates how using vibrato sparingly and ornamentally (as in Beethoven's day) in the fugue can render this transition more striking.[7]

BEETHOVEN AND HIS LISTENERS: CONVERSATIONS AND SILENCE

Why would Beethoven want to write a string quartet that demanded such sustained, challenging, attentive listening (for around 40 uninterrupted minutes)? Beethoven's conversations books offer help with this question, and generally make a fascinating study for anyone interested in his late works and nineteenth-century concert life. They contradict the traditional idea that Beethoven became increasingly "cut off" from reality as his deafness progressed, a belief that starts in earnest with Wagner. The conversation books show Beethoven clearly thirsty for knowledge about performers, listeners, and reception in his milieu; he was eager to take part as fully as he could, asking his immediate circle about the popularity and effect on the public of his latest works. So, for example, after the 1825 premiere of the String Quartet in A minor, Op. 132, the violinist Holz reported to Beethoven:

It was completely full, and the *trio* as well as the *quartet* in particular were very much applauded; it also went together very well and Linke played better than ever. It was too crowded to hear much; but this much I did hear, that many passages were accompanied by exclamations, and upon leaving many people spoke of the beauty of the new quartet. For this reason Schuppanzigh wants to play it again in 14 days. [8]

This and other evidence suggest that audiences at Viennese quartet performances in the 1820s needed a jolt out of complacency or some violation of the status quo to get them to listen attentively: they were used to applauding between movements, calling for repeats of passages they liked, and generally using the occasion to socialize and chat. Beethoven was making a bold statement when offering such demanding music to an audience ill-equipped by habit to listen to it. On the same occasion that Holz discussed with Beethoven where and how the performers were to tune in Op. 131 (see Chapter 3), he also tried to make a joke out of the audience's tendency to chat between movements: "The conversation between one piece (Stück) and the next is never so witty that it could make a relevant intermezzo. / I mean the listener's conversation between pieces."[9] Beethoven's new kind of writing was demanding a new kind of audience.

The conversation books also reveal Beethoven's almost obsessive reluctance to allow the Schuppanzigh players to get their hands on the score of Op. 131 before the performance. This might be puzzling: surely prior access to the score would have given the players the time they needed to study this very complex work before its premier. Other conversations reveal that Beethoven was aiming to have the quartet premiered in another center, namely Berlin, and by another string quartet.[10] The Schuppanzigh players protested, and, apparently ignoring Beethoven's strictures, started to make plans to perform the work in a different room from usual and outside the main series.[11] But in the end Beethoven's wishes were met, albeit after his lifetime: the first performance was given outside Vienna, by the Müller brothers. Thus Op. 131 was the only one of Beethoven's last quartets that did not receive its first performance from the Schuppanzigh quartet. Apparently this exception was due to Beethoven's perception of the work's particular difficulties in terms of performance and reception, and his desire to have it properly understood.

There is further evidence suggesting why Beethoven might have been eager to have the quartet premiered away from his home turf. The conversation books show us that Nos. 2 and 4 of Op. 130 were repeated at the premier in Vienna, by the Schuppanzigh Quartet, implying a rapturous reception by the audience.[12] The reviews reveal to us, nevertheless, that Op. 130's first performance was a disappointment, because the public protested against the finale and the critics disliked it, one saying, for example, that it was like Chinese to him.[13] This spurred Beethoven to compose a new finale in November 1826. But meanwhile he completed Op. 131 and in this work was in no sense "retreating" before or conceding anything to audience behavior; indeed he seemed to be trying to reform it, and seemed to partly blame the Schuppanzigh performance for the mixed reception.

With his emphasis on "a new kind of part writing" in Op. 131, Beethoven was pressing onwards with compositional implications he had been developing in Op. 133. The *Kullak* sketchbook shows that Beethoven was working on ideas for Op. 131 directly after Op. 133. Winter notes a progression: "The sketches up to folio 10r in *Kullak* suggest that the composer proceeded directly from the *Grosse Fuge* to the opening fugue of Op. 131, as if the profound catharsis of the former had released the serene lyricism of the latter."[14] But with an opening fugue, rather than a fugal finale, he was inverting the traditional order, making a striking statement about this work vis-à-vis the entire quartet-writing tradition. By using a fugue at the opening, and following through rigorously on its implications for "equality" in seven extremely various movements, Beethoven demanded a level of attention at least equal to that needed by Op. 130 played together with its original conclusion, the Grosse Fuge.

Beethoven's C-sharp minor quartet can be understood as part of a drive, on the part of certain composers, performers, publishers, and critics, to instill a valuing of sustained, attentive listening. Weber credits this concerted effort with limited but gradual success: "The most important development in the nature of musical listening during the first half of the 19th century did not come about in actual behavior but rather in the *rise of an ideology* by which to reform it."[15] Beethoven was among Viennese composers who called for a change in listening habits. Performers and critics also tried to adjust audiences' behavior at public and semi-public concerts in the early nineteenth century: influential figures such as Schuppanzigh, who tried programming all-string-quartet concerts, and reviewers for the *Wiener Theater-Zeitung* and Viennese *Allgemeine musikalische Zeitung* in the 1810s and 20s, maintained that attentive listening was especially important for string quartets.[16] These people did not necessarily endorse *silent* listening, which was hardly the norm at this point. And although their dissemination of ideas about desirable audience behavior contributed to the rise of an ideology enjoining change in this respect, their attempts to change listeners' behavior were not necessarily successful.

However, the climate in Vienna meant that Beethoven and Schuppanzigh could not enjoy much success with this project. Beethoven evidently wanted to trial his courageous new work in a fresh context, with fresh eyes, ears, and hands. Elsewhere, conditions were more conducive; for example in London, John Ella was soon to be successfully marketing all-quartet subscription concerts.[17] Still, a full appreciation of the plenitude of Op. 131, on Beethoven's own terms, was largely restricted to connoisseurs—listeners like Schumann, Schubert, and Marx. Not all of Op. 131's early champions were German or British. Consider Berlioz, who exemplifies Romantic ideals and "Romantic" listening—if this is taken to mean deeply engaged, attentive listening (see Chapter 2).

REARRANGING LISTENING CULTURE: FOUR-HAND ARRANGEMENTS AND SCORES

The "Romantic listener" does not represent a nineteenth-century norm, far less the norm in Beethoven's Vienna. But silent attention was starting to take hold, thanks not only to the people listed above, but also to the possession and study of scores, which now promoted the understanding of listening as an act separate from performance. The listener was now directed to the notes on the page as an encoding of pure sonority, not only to the act of performance; and the score-carrying listener was now showing himself (usually) or herself (sometimes) to be a connoisseur listener. We have seen that scores of Op. 131 were welcomed by connoisseurs and critics. The score was the new currency of middle-class citizens, with pretensions to ownership of the public musical sphere, including its repositories of knowledge. Carl Friedrich Pohl observed connoisseurs reading miniature scores at concerts in the early nineteenth century.[18] Berlioz reports the same from France in the 1830s, while the *Illustrated London News* shows that connoisseurs were bringing their scores to concerts of Beethoven quartets in the 1840s (Figure 5.2). This practice demonstrates an evolving conception of the musical work: silent score study would gradually displace (although not entirely replace) the hands-on reception and construction of the musical work via performance in the home.

With Beethoven's late quartets, the genre had already moved decisively into the hands of professionals as far as performance was concerned, and so into the concert hall. But certain arrangements of Beethoven's late works adapted these works for a broader audience than was originally intended; such arrangements can be seen as efforts to make the work in question comprehensible, or at least playable, in a domestic setting, and to allow it to be heard by listeners of limited social, economic, or educational capital. These arrangements were also related to the shift to more attentive listening. Reviewers of the time suggested playing through the piano arrangements or studying the scores of

FIGURE 5.2 *Illustrated London News* (1846); listener John Ella is labeled together with the players: Henry Vieuxtemps (violin 1), Monsieur Deloffre (violin 2), Henry Lockey Hill (viola), and Alfredo Piatti (cello).

the late quartets in order to understand them.[19] Op. 135 was available almost immediately in a four-hand piano arrangement by A. B. Marx, as were all of the late quartets except Opp. 130 and 131. In 1858, Schott released an edition of a four-hand arrangement of the C-sharp minor quartet by Franz Xaver Gleichauf; there followed four-hand arrangements by Louis Winkler in 1865 and Hugo Ulrich around 1890. Karl Müller Berghaus orchestrated the work in the late nineteenth century.

These arrangements are important in the reception history of Op. 131 because they point us to a crucial transition in the way the work was conceived and experienced. Some of these arrangements, notably that of Ulrich, are concerned with retaining the main conception of the work in terms of its aesthetic, but translating it into something readily playable. The concern is not so much with note-for-note fidelity to Beethoven's original, but rather with "getting inside" the work's aesthetic—hearing it, and experiencing it as if the two performers were recreating it on the spot. Other arrangers leaned toward the new score-focused conception of the musical work, apparent not only in producing scores themselves, but also in the practice of score analysis that arose contemporaneously (see Chapter 1). In such arrangements, fidelity to the original meant retaining the notes and textures of the original, and laying the work out in a clearly structured way so as to emulate the overview of a full score.

Gleichauf's arrangement offers a useful point of comparison with that of Ulrich. Ulrich created what could be called a four-hand piano "performance edition" of Op. 131, giving distinct functions to Primo and Secondo. This approach is immediately apparent in the opening fugue, where the Secondo waits seven bars for the Primo to deliver the first and second violin material, and from then on adds textural thickening to each part, as well as pedal, so that each is relatively self-contained and is easily within the reach of amateurs. By contrast, Gleichauf produces a four-hand piano "score edition" of Op. 131. He has the Secondo enter with the second violin's material in bar 4, and in general shows a concern to retain a sense of the distinct voices, as in a score. Most telling, though, is each arranger's treatment of page turns and the cadenza-like passages—moments that require a subtle sense of flow as well as articulation. Here Ulrich and his publisher Peters retain the flow between *Stücke* by avoiding page turns during the transitions. Gleichauf and his publisher Schott take the opposite approach, undermining continuity at transitions by placing each on a page turn. Exceptionally, No. 7 appears directly after No. 6 on the same page and without a number label in both arrangements. This is because both Gleichauf and his publisher Peters considered No. 6 to be an introduction to No. 7, not a piece in its own right—as did Tovey, and before him Helm, who heard No. 6 as a "recitative-like introduction" (*rezitativische verklingenden Einleitung*)(Example 5.1).[20]

In another effort to turn the work into a score, Gleichauf and his publisher placed little ossia indications in the Secondo at points where the primo has cadenzas (Nos. 3 and 4). But the most explicit instance of such "scoring" of Op. 131, exceeding even the quartet score editions themselves,

EXAMPLE 5.1   Primo part of Gleichauf's four-hand piano arrangement of Beethoven's Op. 131, No. 6, showing the *attacca* transition to No. 7, without label.

EXAMPLE 5.2   Berghaus's scoring of Op. 131 for full symphony orchestral, final bars.

is the full orchestral score version produced by Berghaus (Example 5.2). Although Beethoven might have appreciated the silence that this massive "C-sharp minor symphony" would command of listeners in the late nineteenth-century concert hall, he would surely have found something essential lost in translation, especially if performed by one of the increasingly massive orchestras of the day. The large complement of brass and winds is more suitable for Bruckner than for Beethoven, but it is entirely in keeping with the late nineteenth-century image of Beethoven's late works as massive, complex, and masterful. The finale is rendered as a weighty goal attained by sheer sonic power, rather than an oddly inconclusive final utterance. Absent in this arrangement, is the greater room for performers' and listeners' interpretations, and any sense of finely-wrought voice in the work, whose infinite shades of affect and delicate turns of phrase had been the hallmarks of chamber music to the end of Beethoven's life.

EPILOGUE

O P. 131 HAS BEEN read as a tragic, deafness-induced chaos or as an innovative triumph taking the potential of music closer to the sublime and perhaps the divine. Was it an over-ambitious jumbled patchwork? Or was it a deliberate composition of various *Stücke* to achieve a whole wherein exultation pays tribute to the depth that melancholia adds to the human condition? Might the *riss* that is Op. 131 be read through a Lacanian lens as the Lack that motivates longing and action? How should a reading of this work prioritize the cerebral, the kinaesthetic, and the anagogic? Important is that the questions remain.

Music is both personal and social. Op. 131 is constructed by the performers and by the listening audience, and the listening and reading audience. But we could also say that

Beethoven's String Quartet in C-sharp Minor, Op. 131. Nancy November, Oxford University Press.
© Oxford University Press 2021. DOI: 10.1093/oso/9780190059200.003.0007

the work constructs (or at least develops) performers and audience. Over two centuries, Op. 131 has been placed on a continuum between fragmentation and unity. Where we—especially more recent scholars—have tried to enforce the latter reading, we can return to earlier ideas, including those of Beethoven's day, to open up perceptions, performances, and questions of the work today. Beethoven's multivalent compositional methodology pushes the boundaries: conventions are teasingly flaunted; and innovations rouse listeners from passive reception to active involvement, challenging us to improvise the work anew on each hearing.

NOTES

CHAPTER 1

1   See Emily Anderson (ed. and trans.), *The Letters of Beethoven* (1961; repr. New York: Norton, 1985), 3, no. 1498:1295, n. 2; see also Sieghard Brandenburg (ed.), *Ludwig van Beethoven. Briefwechsel: Gesamtausgabe* (Munich: Henle, 1996–98), 6, no. 2187:269.

2   Krista M. Knittel, "Wagner, Deafness, and the Reception of Beethoven's Late Style," *Journal of the American Musicological Society* 51, no. 1 (1998), pp. 49–82; see also Knittel, "From Chaos to History: The Reception of Beethoven's Late Quartets," PhD diss., Princeton University, 1992.

3   Richard Wagner, *Beethoven* (Leipzig: Fritzsch, 1870), p. 36; Edward Dannreuther (ed. and trans.), *Beethoven. By Richard Wagner. With a supplement from the philosophical works of Arnold Schopenhauer* (London: Reeves, 1880), p. 55, mentions the symphonies in A and F (Nos. 6 and 7) as being written at a time of "total deafness" (1808 and 1811–12, respectively); so the "late period" belongs in what we now consider the end of the "middle period."

4   Gustav Nottebohm, "Arbeiten zum Quartett in Cis-moll," *Allgemeine musikalische Zeitung* 5, no. 4 (January 26, 1870), p. 26. Repr. *Beethoveniana* (Leipzig: Rieter-Biedermann, 1827), p. 54.

5   K. M. Knittel, "'Late,' Last, and Least: On Being Beethoven's Quartet in F Major, Op. 135," *Music and Letters* 87, no. 1 (2006), pp. 16–51.

6   Wagner, *Beethoven* (Leipzig: Fritzsch, 1870), p. 36; Dannreuther (ed. and trans.), *Beethoven*, pp. 55–56.

7   Wagner, *Beethoven*, p. 38; Dannreuther (ed.), *Beethoven*, p. 59.

8   Wagner, *Beethoven*, p. 40; Dannreuther (ed.), *Beethoven*, p. 61.

9   See my "Picturing Nineteenth-Century String Quartet Listeners," *Music in Art* 41, nos. 1–2 (2016), pp. 18–19.

10 On the nineteenth-century reception of Haydn as "father" or "papa," see especially Ludwig Nohl, *Die Geschichtliche Entwickelung der Kammermusik und ihre Bedeutung für den Musiker* (Braunschweig: F. Vieweg und Sohn, 1885), especially Ch. 2, "Der Vater des Quartetts," pp. 67–82; see also Leon Botstein, "The Consequences of Presumed Innocence: The Nineteenth-century Reception of Joseph Haydn," in W. Dean Sutcliffe (ed.), *Haydn Studies* (Cambridge: Cambridge University Press, 1998), pp. 1–34.

11 Wagner, *Beethoven*, pp. 15–16; Dannreuther (ed.), *Beethoven*, pp. 24–25.

12 Wagner, *Beethoven*, p. 35; Dannreuther (ed.), *Beethoven*, p. 54.

13 These conversation books are blank booklets that Beethoven carried with him from 1818 onwards, so that his acquaintances could note their sides of conversations, while he answered (mostly) aloud.

14 Joseph Kerman, *The Beethoven Quartets* (New York, NY: A. A. Knopf, 1967), p. 334.

15 Theodor Helm, *Beethoven's Streichquartette. Verusch einer technischen Analyse dieser Werke im Zusammenhang mit ihrem geistigen Gehalt* (Leipzig: Fritsch, 1885). The comments first appeared in the *Musikalisches Wochenblatt*, 4, no. 40–8, no. 39 (October 3, 1873–September 21, 1882).

16 Helm, *Beethoven's Streichquartette*, p. 165.

17 Ibid., pp. 233–4.

18 On this topic, see Scott Burnham, *Beethoven Hero* (Princeton, NJ: Princeton University Press, 2000), especially Ch. 3 ("Institutional Values: Beethoven and the Theorists"), pp. 66–111.

19 Helm, *Beethoven's Streichquartette*, p. 233.

20 Ibid., pp. 261–2.

21 Ibid., p. 117.

22 See my *Beethoven's Theatrical Quartets: Opp. 59, 74 and 95* (Cambridge: Cambridge University Press, 2013), p. 4.

23 Edward Dannreuther, "Beethoven and His Works: A Study," *Macmillan's Magazine* 34 (July, 1876), p. 197.

24 Joseph de Marliave, *Les quatuors de Beethoven*, ed. Jean Escarra (Paris: Librairie Félix Alcan, 1925), p. 346, trans. Hilda Andrews, *Beethoven's Quartets* (London: Oxford University Press, 1928), p. 322. Marliave repeated Helm virtually verbatim without acknowledgement.

25 Kerman, *The Beethoven Quartets*, p. 330.

26 Donald Francis Tovey, "Some Aspects of Beethoven's Art Forms," *Music and Letters* 8, no. 2 (1927), pp. 131–55.

27 Ibid., p. 133.

28 See Michael Allen Warner's more detailed discussion, with a focus on Tovey: "What is 'Normal'?: A Beethovenian Reconsideration of Some of Tovey's Aesthetic Principles," MMus diss., University of Illinois, 2010.

29 See Chapter 4 for further discussion of the concept of "Stücke" applied to this context.

30 Tovey, "Some Aspects of Beethoven's Art Forms," pp. 148–51.

31 Lewis Lockwood, *Beethoven: The Music and the Life* (New York, NY: Norton, 2005), pp. 470–1.

32 Tovey, "Some Aspects of Beethoven's Art Forms," p. 151.

33 Vincent d'Indy s.v., "Beethoven, Ludwig van: 1770–1827," in *Cobbett's Cyclopedic Survey of Chamber Music*, ed. Walter Willson Cobbett (London: Oxford University Press, 1929; repr. 1963), 1:105.

34 Leonard G. Ratner, *The Beethoven String Quartets: Compositional Strategies and Rhetoric* (Stanford CA: Stanford Bookstore, 1995), p. 238.

35 Tovey, "Some Aspects of Beethoven's Art Forms," p. 153.

36 Paul Bekker, *Beethoven* (Berlin: Schuster & Loeffler, 1911).

37 Daniel Gregory Mason, *The Quartets of Beethoven* (New York: Oxford University Press, 1949), p. 241 (emphasis added).

38 Mason, *The Quartets of Beethoven*, pp. 265–6.

39 Tovey, "Some Aspects of Beethoven's Art Forms," p. 153.

40 Joseph Kerman, "Beethoven's Opus 131 and the Uncanny," *19th-Century Music* 25, nos. 2–3 (2001–02), p. 156.

41 J. W. N. Sullivan, *Beethoven: His Spiritual Development* (New York: Knopf, 1927), p. 243.

42 Robert Winter, *Compositional Origins of Beethoven's Op. 131* (Ann Arbor, MI: UMI Research Press, 1982), p. 146.

43 Tovey, "Some Aspects of Beethoven's Art Forms," p. 131.

44 Mason, *The Quartets of Beethoven*, p. 254.

45 See note 23.

46 Kerman, *The Beethoven Quartets*, p. 341.

47 Mason, *The Quartets of Beethoven*, p. 262.

48 Ibid., p. 341.

49 Ibid.

50 Kerman, *The Beethoven Quartets*, p. 348. See also my comments on Kerman's metaphors in connection with the middle-period quartets in my *Beethoven's Theatrical Quartets*, p. 4, n. 11.

51 Kerman, *The Beethoven Quartets*, p. 349.

52 Ibid., p. 29.

53 Ibid., p. 331.

54 Theodor Adorno, *Beethoven: The Philosophy of Music (Fragments and Texts)*, ed. Rolf Tiedemann and trans. Edmund Jephcott (Stanford, CA: Stanford University Press, 1998), Ch. 10 ("Late Work without Late Style"), pp. 138–53.

55 Ibid., p. 125 (emphasis original).

56 William Kinderman, "Beethoven's Last Quartets: Threshold to a Fourth Creative Period?," in *The String Quartets of Beethoven*, ed. William Kinderman (Urbana, IL: University of Illinois Press, 2006), pp. 279–321 (containing essays from a conference held at the University of Victoria, Canada, March 2000).

57 Kerman, "Opus 131 and the Uncanny," p. 156.

58 Ibid., p. 156.

59 Lawrence Kramer, "The Musicology of the Future," *Repercussions* 1, no. 1 (1992), pp. 5–18.

60 Gary Tomlinson, "Gary Tomlinson Responds," *Current Musicology* 53 (1994), p. 38.

61 See Jeffrey Swinkin, "The Middle/Late Style Dialectic: Problematizing Adorno's Theory of Beethoven," *Journal of Musicology* 30, no. 3 (2013), p. 291.

62 Kinderman, "Beethoven's Last Quartets," p. 316.

63 Ibid., p. 310.

64 Ibid., p. 314.

65 Gerd Indorf, *Beethovens Streichquartette: Kulturgeschichtliche Aspekte und Werkinterpretation* (Freiburg: Rombach Verlag, 2004), pp. 451–79.

66 Amanda Glauert, "The Double Perspective in Beethoven's Op. 131," *19th-Century Music* 4, no. 2 (1980), pp. 117–8; see also Chapter 3, note 26.

CHAPTER 2

1 Stasis in reception can be studied, as well as change in reception, as in Hans Heinrich Eggebrecht's "reception constants"; Hans Heinrich Eggebrecht, *Zur Geschichte der Beethoven-Rezeption: Beethoven* (Wiesbaden: Akademie der Wissenschaften und der Literatur, 1972).

2 See, in particular, James Parakilas, "The Power of Domestication in the Lives of Musical Canon," *Repercussions* 4, no. 1 (1995), pp. 5–25.

3 Wilhelm von Lenz, *Beethoven: Eine Kunststudie* (Hamburg: Hoffmann & Campe, 1855–60), 5:217.

4 Dannreuther (ed.), *Beethoven*, p. 62. Wagner quotes from Faust here.

5 Tovey, "Some Aspects of Beethoven's Art Forms," p. 149; Kerman, *The Beethoven Quartets*, p. 333.

6 On "emplotment" and the construction of historical narratives, see Hayden White, *Metahistory: The Historical Imagination in Nineteenth-Century Europe* (Baltimore, MD and London: John Hopkins University Press, 1973).

7 William Kinderman, *Beethoven* (Oxford and New York, NY: Oxford University Press, 2009), p. 356.

8 White, *Metahistory*, p. 8.

9 Michael Steinberg, "The Late Quartets," in *The Beethoven Quartet Companion*, ed. Robert Winter and Robert Martin (Berkeley and Los Angeles, LA: University of California Press, 1994), p. 264.

10 For an excerpt, see "Band of Brothers E09 Why We Fight—Beethoven," available at https://www.youtube.com/watch?v=5YD-PcQ-jJM, accessed April 23, 2020.

11 Adolf Bernhard Marx, *Leben und Schaffen* (Berlin: Janke, 1859), 2:334. Marx uses the number Op. 132 for this work.

12 "Evaluations," *Berliner allgemeine musikalische Zeitung* 5, no. 49 (December 3, 1828), pp. 467–8; Robin Wallace, trans., *The Critical Reception of Beethoven's Compositions by His German Contemporaries Op. 126 to WoO 140* (Boston, MA: Center for Beethoven Research Boston University, 2018), p. 61.

13 Leon Botstein, "The Patrons and Publics of the Quartets: Music, Culture, and Society in Beethoven's Vienna," in *The Beethoven Quartet Companion*, ed. Robert Winter and Robert Martin (Berkeley and Los Angeles, LA: University of California Press, 1994), p. 105.

14 Robert Schumann, *Music and Musicians, Essays and Criticisms*, trans. Frances Malone Ritter (Oxford: Oxford University Press, 1877), p. 391.

15 See Brandenburg, ed., *Ludwig van Beethoven. Briefwechsel* 6, no. 2180:265.

16 Ibid., no. 2187, p. 269.

17 Lenz, *Beethoven: Eine Kunststudie*, 5:217.

18 Marx, *Leben und Schaffen*, 2:334.

19 Ignaz von Seyfried, "III. Das Quatuor," *Cäcilia* 9, no. 36 (1828), p. 241; trans. in Stefan Kunze, *Ludwig van Beethoven, die Werke im Spiegel seiner Zeit: gesammelte Konzertberichte und Rezensionen bis 1830*, ed. Stefan Kunze, Theodor Schmid, Andreas Traub, and Gerda Burkhard (Laaber: Laaber, 1987), p. 576, available at https://www.digizeitschriften.de/dms/img/?PID=PPN4728852940009|log51&physid=phys257#navi, accessed August 24, 2020; on Seyfried as a reviewer of Beethoven's music, see Klaus Martin Kopitz, "Beethoven und seine Rezensenten: ein Blick hinter die Kulissen der *Allgemeinen musikalischen Zeitung*," in *Beethoven und der Leipziger Musikverlag Breitkopf & Härtel: "ich gebe Ihrer Handlung den Vorzug vor allen andern*," ed. Nicole Kämpken and Michael Ladenburger (Bonn: Beethoven-Haus, 2007), pp. 158–9.

20 Marx, *Leben und Schaffen*, 2:334.

21 Brandenburg, ed., *Ludwig van Beethoven. Briefwechsel* 5, no. 1881, pp. 368–9; the letter is also reproduced in *Cäcilia* 6, no. 24 (1827), p. 311, available at https://archive.org/details/bubgbZ2cPAAAAYAAJ/page/n319, accessed August 24, 2020.

22 See especially Megan Ross, "The Critical Reception of Beethoven's String Quartet in C# Minor, Op. 131," PhD diss., The University of North Carolina at Chapel Hill, 2019, in particular pp. 100–27; and as I have also argued in my *Beethoven's Theatrical Quartets*, especially pp. 244–6.

23 *Revue musicale* 7 (series 2, vol. 1) (February 6, 1830), p. 280, available at https://archive.org/details/revuemusicale18307pari/page/280/mode/2up, accessed August 24, 2020; Kunze, *Ludwig van Beethoven*, p. 581.

24 Alexander Oulibicheff, *Beethoven, ses critiques et ses glossateurs* (Leipzig: F. A. Brockhaus and Paris: Jules Gavelot, 1857), pp. 257 and 259.

25 V. Weiler, *Cäcilia* 9, no. 33 (1828), p. 46; Kunze, *Ludwig van Beethoven*, p. 573; Wallace, *The Critical Reception*, p. 44. On the identity of this reviewer see Wallace p. 44, n. 1.

26 Weiler, *Cäcilia* 9, no. 33 (1828), p. 46; Kunze, *Ludwig van Beethoven*, p. 573; Wallace, *The Critical Reception*, p. 44.

27 Friedrich Rochlitz, "Auf Veranlassung von . . . ," *Allgemeine musikalische Zeitung* 30, no. 31 (July 30, 1828), col. 506, available at https://opacplus.bsb-muenchen.de/Vta2/bsb10528029/bsb:4114350?page=5, accessed August 24, 2020; Kunze, *Ludwig van Beethoven*, p. 570; Wallace, *The Critical Reception*, pp. 56–7.

28 See especially Peter Bloom, "Critical Reaction to Beethoven in France: François-Joseph Fétis," *Revue Belge De Musicologie/Belgisch Tijdschrift voor Muziekwetenschap* 26, no. 27 (1972), pp. 67–83; and Beate Angelika Kraus, *Beethoven-Rezeption in Frankreich. Von ihren Anfängen bis zum Unergang des Second Empire* (Bonn: Beethoven-Haus, 2001).

29 For a detailed reading of Hoffmann's Beethoven criticism, relating his the language to ideas of the Prussian reform movement and political Romanticism, see Stephen Rumph, "A Kingdom Not of this World," *19th-Century Music* 19, no. 1 (1995), pp. 50–67.

30 Seyfried, "III. Das Quatuor," p. 241; Kunze, *Ludwig van Beethoven*, p. 576.

31 Seyfried, "III. Das Quatuor," p. 243; Kunze, *Ludwig van Beethoven*, p. 580.

32 Ludwig van Beethoven, *Streichquartette III*, ed. Emil Platen and Rainer Cadenbach (Munich: G. Henle, 2015), p. 18.

33 See Grita Herre and Karl-Heinz Köhler, eds., *Ludwig van Beethovens Konversationshefte*, 11 vols. (Leipzig: Deutscher Verlag für Musik, 1968–2001), 8:259.

34 Rochlitz, "Auf Veranlassung von . . . ," cols. 507–8; Kunze, *Ludwig van Beethoven*, pp. 570–1; Wallace, *The Critical Reception*, pp. 57–8.

35 Anon., "Kurze Beurtheilungen," *Allgemeine Musikzeitung zur Beförderung der theoretischen und praktischen Tonkunst für Musiker und für Freunde der Musik überhaupt* 2, no. 15 (February 20, 1828), col. 119, available at https://books.google.de/books?id=A-gsAAAAYAAJ&printsec=frontcover&hl=de#v=onepage&q&f=false, p. 36, accessed August 24, 2020; Kunze, *Ludwig van Beethoven*, p. 560; Wallace, *The Critical Reception*, p. 43.

36 Rochlitz, "Auf Veranlassung von . . . ," col. 501; Kunze, *Ludwig van Beethoven*, p. 567; Wallace, *The Critical Reception*, p. 54.

37 Rochlitz, "Auf Veranlassung von . . . ," col. 502; Kunze, *Ludwig van Beethoven*, pp. 567–8; Wallace, *The Critical Reception*, p. 54.

38 Rochlitz, "Auf Veranlassung von . . . ," col. 509; Kunze, *Ludwig van Beethoven*, p. 572; Wallace, *The Critical Reception*, p. 58.

39 *Revue musicale* 7, pp. 281–2; Kunze, *Ludwig van Beethoven*, p. 582.

40 Reproduced in Gérard Condé, ed., *Hector Berlioz. Cauchemars et Passions* (Paris: Jean Claude Lattès, 1981), pp. 58–9.

41 *Berliner allgemeine musikalische Zeitung* 7, no. 17 (April 24, 1830), p. 135.

42 Mary Hunter, "The Most Interesting Genre of Music: Performance, Sociability and Meaning in the Classical String Quartets, 1800–1830," *Nineteenth-Century Music Review* 9, no. 1 (2012), p. 61. But Hunter notes further that the German-language press also occasionally described quartet concerts as if they were violin solos. The Bohrer Quartet, which included the brothers Anton (1783–1852) and Max Bohrer (1785–1867), performed the Op. 59 set, Op. 127, Op. 130, Op. 131, and Op. 132 during 1830 and 1831.

43 See the 1845 edition of Fétis's treatise *La musique mise à la porte de tout le monde* (Paris: Paulin and E. Duverger, 1834), p. 335, available at https://gallica.bnf.fr/ark:/12148/bpt6k96882331.texteImage, accessed August 24, 2020.

44 See note 17.

CHAPTER 3

1 Rochlitz, "Auf Veranlassung von . . . ," col. 506; Kunze, *Ludwig van Beethoven*, p. 570; trans. Wallace, *The Critical Reception*, p. 56.

2 Robin Wallace, *Hearing Beethoven: A Story of Musical Loss and Discovery* (Chicago, IL: University of Chicago Press, 2018), pp. 187–8 (my emphasis).

3 Helm, *Beethovens Streichquartette*, p. 217; this statement is also discussed in some detail in William Drabkin, "The Cello Part in Beethoven's Late Quartets," *Beethoven Forum* 7 (1999), especially pp. 45–6.

4 On this subject, see also my *Beethoven's Theatrical Quartets*, pp. 8–24.

5 This is a reference from Virgil: "The women of Camoena [muses] love it alternately."

6 Johann Conrad Wilhelm Petiscus ("P. "), "Ueber Quartettmusik," *Allgemeine musicalische Zeitung* 12, no. 33 (May 16, 1810), col. 516.

7 Koch, *Versuch einer Anleitung zur Composition* (Rudolstadt and Leipzig: Böhme, 1782–93), 3:326 and 433–43.

8 Anon., "Recension," *Allgemeine musicalische Zeitung* 10, no. 28 (April 6, 1808), col. 435.

9 Adolph Bernhard Marx, "Quatuor für zwei Violinen, Viola und Violincell von Beethoven . . . ," *Berliner allgemeine musikalische Zeitung* 5, no. 49 (December 3, 1828), p. 467.

10 See my analysis in "Register in Haydn's String Quartets: Four Case Studies," *Music Analysis* 26, no. 3 (2007), pp. 298 and 301.

11 Discussed at length by William Drabkin in *A Reader's Guide to Haydn's Early String Quartets* (Westport, CT: Greenwood Press, 2000), pp. 51–68.

12 On this subject, see Janet M. Levy, *The Quatuor Concertant in Paris in the Latter Half of the Eighteenth Century*, PhD diss., Stanford University, 1971; and Barbara R. Hanning, "Conversation and Musical Style in the Late Eighteenth-Century Parisian Salon," *Eighteenth-Century Studies* 22, no. 4 (1989), pp. 512–28.

13 On this topic, see John Irving, *Mozart: The "Haydn" Quartets* (New York: Cambridge University Press, 1998), especially p. 75.

14 See also Mark Evan Bonds, "The Sincerest Form of Flattery? Mozart's 'Haydn' Quartets and the Question of Influence," *Studi Musicali* 22, no. 2 (1993), pp. 365–410.

15 The phrase is discussed by Gretchen A. Wheelock, among others: *Haydn's Ingenious Jesting with Art: Contexts of Musical Wit and Humor* (New York, NY: Schirmer, 1992), p. 96.

16 Adolf Sandberger, "Zur Geschichte des Haydnschen Streichquartetts," *Altbayerische Monatsschrift* 2 (1900), pp. 63–4; rev. repr. in Adolf Sandberger, *Ausgewahlte Aufsätze zur Musikgeschichte* (Munich: Drei Masken, 1921), 1:262–3; trans. James Webster, *Haydn's "Farewell" Symphony and the Idea of Classical Style* (Cambridge: Cambridge University Press, 1991), p. 342 (emphasis original).

17 Mary Hunter, "The Most Interesting Genre of Music," especially pp. 59–66.

18 See my *Beethoven's Theatrical Quartets*, pp. 8–24 and 249–50.

19 Drabkin, *A Reader's Guide*, p. 52; see Tovey, "Some Aspects of Beethoven's Art Forms," p. 135.

20 Helm, *Beethovens Streichquartette*, p. 117.

21 Lawrence Vittes, "Straight from the Heart: A String Player's Guide to the Late Quartets," *Strings* 25, no. 9 (2011), p. 48.

22 Ibid., p. 49.

23 See Mary Hunter, "To Play as if from the Soul of the Composer: The Idea of the Performer in Early Romantic Aesthetics," *Journal of the American Musicological Society* 58, no. 2 (2005), especially pp. 366–7.

24 Lawrence Vittes, "NYC Quartet Approaches a Chamber Classic with 'A Clean Slate'," *Strings* 26, no. 206 (2012), p. 34 (emphasis added).

25 Vittes, "Straight from the Heart," p. 47.

26 Glauert, "The Double Perspective in Beethoven's Op. 131," p. 117.

27 Ibid.

28 *Ludwig van Beethoven: Ein Skizzenbuch aus dem Jahre 1809 (Landsberg 5)*, ed. Clemens Brenneis (Bonn: Beethoven-Haus, 1993), 1:24.

29 Seow-Chin Ong, "Aspects of the Genesis of Beethoven's String Quartet in F minor, Op. 95," in *The String Quartets of Beethoven*, ed. Kinderman, p. 143.

30 William Kinderman, "The Evolution of Beethoven's Late Style: Another 'New Path' after 1824?," *Beethoven Forum* 8 (2000), p. 96; Winter, *Compositional Origins*, pp. 113–34.

31 See for example Albert S. Bregman, *Auditory Scene Analysis: The Perceptual Organization of Sound* (Cambridge, MA: MIT Press, 1990).

32 Wallace, *Hearing Beethoven*, p. 154 (emphasis added).

33 Ibid., p. 173.

34 Ibid., pp. 163–4.

35 Ibid., p. 174.

36 Ibid., p. 175.

37 See, for example, Pierre Baillot, *L'art du violon. Nouvelle Méthode* (Paris: Depot Central de la Musique, [1834]), pp. 140–4.

38 "Sul ponticello" means that the performer bows near the bridge to bring out the higher harmonics in a given tone, hence producing a nasal tone; on the term "non-ligato," see Robert Martin, "The Late Quartets," in *The Beethoven Quartet Companion*, pp. 113–5.

39 Seyfried, "III. Das Quatuor," p. 243; Kunze, *Ludwig van Beethoven*, p. 580.

40 Vittes, "Straight from the Heart," p. 48.

41 Anon., "Nachrichten. Wien," *Allgemeine musikalische Zeitung* 28, no. 19 (May 10, 1826), col. 311.

42 Adolf Bernhard Marx, "Recension: L. v. Beethoven Overtüre et Entr'actes de la Tragédie Egmont . . . ," *Berliner allgemeine musikalische Zeitung* 4, no. 25 (June 20, 1827), p. 194.

43 For example Kerman, *The Beethoven Quartets*, p. 341; Winter, *Compositional Origins*, p. 137.

44 Winter, *Compositional Origins*, p. 213.

45 Ibid.

46 Ibid., pp. 216 and 238.

47 Glauert, "The Double Perspective," p. 119.

48 Helm, *Beethovens Streichquartette*, p. 242.

49 See Ratner, *The Beethoven String Quartets*, p. 250.

50 Herre and Köhler (eds.), *Ludwig van Beethovens Konversationshefte*, 8:163.

51 First violin can tune the upper two strings in bars 162–3 and 173–4; second violin can tune the two lower strings in bars 178–9; viola can tune the two lower strings bars 181–2; and the two middle strings in bars 177–9; while cello can tune the two lower strings in bars 177–9 and 186.

CHAPTER 4

1 Rochlitz, "Auf Veranlassung von . . . ," col. 506; Kunze, *Ludwig van Beethoven*, p. 570; trans. Wallace, *The Critical Reception*, p. 56.

2 Ratner, *The Beethoven String Quartets*, p. 235 (emphasis added).

3 Ibid., p. 236.

4 Barbara Barry, "Invisible Cities and Imaginary Landscapes 'quasi una fantasia': On Beethoven's Op. 131," *The Musical Times* 158, no. 1938 (2017), p. 15.

5 Ibid., p. 16.

6 Indorf *Beethovens Streichquartette*, p. 451; Beethoven, *Streichquartette III*, ed. Platen and Cadenbach, p. 53.

7 Allen Spreight, "Friedrich Schlegel," in *The Stanford Encyclopedia of Philosophy* (2016), ed. Edward N. Zalta, available at https://plato.stanford.edu/archives/win2016/entries/schlegel/, accessed December 9, 2019.

8 Barry, "Invisible Cities," p. 16.

9 Martha B. Helfer (ed.), *Rereading Romanticism* (Amsterdam and Atlanta, GA: Rodopi, 2000), p. 145.

10 David Ferris, *Schumann's* Eichendorff Liederkreis *and the Genre of the Romantic Cycle* (New York, NY: Oxford University Press, 2000), pp. 69–70.

11 Ibid., p. 73.

12 Ibid.

13 See Chapter 1, Mason, *The Quartets of Beethoven*.

14 Ferris, *Schumann's* Eichendorff Liederkreis, p. 70.

15 Karin Bomhoff, *Bildende Kunst und Dichtung. Die Selbstinterpretationen E.T.A. Hoffmanns in der Kunst Jacques Callots und Salvator Rosas* (Freiburg: Rombach, 1999), p. 55. Literary fantasias have been shown to operate musically, too, often seeming to emerge via explicit reference to sound which itself perpetuates otherworldly modes of seeing and knowing. See Francesca Brittan, *Music and Fantasy in the Age of Berlioz* (Cambridge: Cambridge University Press, 2017), p. 3.

16 Anon., "Recension [Op. 74]," *Allgemeine musikalische Zeitung* 13, no. 21 (May 22, 1811), pp. 350–1.

17 John M. Gingerich, *Schubert's Beethoven Project* (Cambridge and New York, NY: Cambridge University Press, 2014), p. 113. See also chapter 3 on the imperative for good *thematische Arbeit* in the string quartet.

18 Petiscus, "Über Quartetmusik," col. 520.

19 Annette Richards, *The Free Fantasia and the Musical Picturesque* (Cambridge: Cambridge University Press, 2001), p. 18.

20 On the emerging conception of "true" string quartets, see my *Beethoven's Theatrical Quartets*, pp. 8–17.

21 Richards, *The Free Fantasia*, p. 18.

22 *Allgemeine musikalische Zeitung* 10, no. 40 (June 30, 1807), p. 725.

23 *Allgemeine musikalische Zeitung* 4, no. 40, no. 16 (August 10, 1802), cols. 650–3.

24 Lenz, *Beethoven: Eine Kunststudie*, 5:215.

25 Helm, *Beethoven's Streichquartette*, p. 234.

26 Trans. in Richards, *The Free Fantasia*, p. 199. See also Fétis's comments on fantasia cited in Chapter 2, at note 43.

27 Amadeus Wendt, "Gedanken über die neuere Tonkunst, und van Beethovens Musik, namentlich dessen Fidelio," *Allgemeine musikalische Zeitung* 17, no. 23 (June 7, 1815), cols. 385–6.

28 Richards, *The Free Fantasia*, p. 191.

29 Richards, *The Free Fantasia*, p. 191.

30 Carl Philipp Emmanuel Bach, *Versuch über die wahre Art das Klavier zu Spielen*, Part II (Berlin: G. W. Winter: 1762), pp. 336–8.

31 Winter, *Compositional Origins*, especially Chapter 6, pp. 113–34.

32 Richards, *The Free Fantasia*, especially Chapter 1, pp. 1–33.

33 See also Tzvetan Todorov, *The Fantastic: A Structural Approach to a Literary Genre*, trans. Richard Howard (Ithaca, NY: Cornell University Press, 1975), p. 42.

34 On this subject, see especially Barry Cooper, "Beethoven and the Double Bar," *Music & Letters* 88, no. 3 (2007), pp. 458–83.

35 See Rey M. Longyear, "Beethoven and Romantic Irony," *Musical Quarterly* 56, no. 4 (1970), pp. 647–64.

36 Helm, *Beethoven's Streichquartette*, p. 234.

37 Richards, *The Free Fantasia*, p. 182.

38 *Allgemeine musikalische Zeitung* 9, no. 27 (April 1, 1807), col. 435.

39 Friedhelm Krummacher, *Das Streichquartett. I. Von Haydn bis Schubert*, *Handbuch der musikalischen Gattungen*, 6 vols. (Bremen: Laaber, 2001), 1:263.

40 Indorf, *Beethovens Streichquartette*, pp. 458–9. See also the literature on Op. 59, No. 1, Scherzo and the "duck/rabbit" phenomenon: Lewis Lockwood, "A Problem of Form: The 'Scherzo' of Beethoven's String Quartet in F major, Op. 59, no. 1," *Beethoven Forum* 2, no. 1 (1993), pp. 85–95.

41 Christian Schubart, *Ideen zu einer Aesthetik der Tonkunst* (Vienna: Degen, 1806), p. 379, available at https://reader.digitale-sammlungen.de/en/fs1/object/display/bsb10599461_00397.html, accessed August 28, 2020.

42 Immanuel Kant, *Beobachtungen über das Gefühl des Schönen und Erhabenen* (Königsberg: Kanter, 1764), p. 33; Kant, *Anthropologie in pragmatischer Hinsicht* (Königsberg: Kanter, 1798), p. 260.

43 Kant, *Beobachtungen*, pp. 33–34; trans. John T. Goldthwait, *Observations on the Feeling of the Beautiful and Sublime* (Berkeley and Los Angeles, CA: University of California Press, 2004), pp. 66–7.

44 *Ueber die Einsamkeit* (1784–1785). For a detailed discussion of Zimmermann's Johann Georg Zimmermann, *Ueber die Einsamkeit*, 2nd ed. (Karlsruhe: Schmieder, 1790), vol. 4. For a detailed discussion of Zimmermann's conceptions of melancholy, see Hans-Jürgen Schings, *Melancholie und Aufklärung: Melancholiker und ihre Kritiker in Erfahrungsseelenkunde und Literatur des 18. Jahrhunderts* (Stuttgart: Springer, 1977), pp. 217–25. The relationship between solitude and melancholy in Zimmermann's writings is discussed in

Wolff Lepenies, *Melancholy and Society*, trans. Jeremy Gaines and Doris Jones (Cambridge, MA: Harvard University Press, 1992), pp. 62–6.

45 Zimmermann, *Ueber die Einsamkeit*, 4:6.

46 Ibid., p. 191.

47 Zimmermann, *Ueber die Einsamkeit*, 3:173.

48 Schubart, *Ideen zu einer*, p. 379.

49 Joseph Leo Koerner, *The Moment of Self-Portraiture in German Renaissance Art* (Chicago, IL: University of Chicago Press, 1993), p. 23.

50 On links between the opening of this movement and the ensuing Allegro, see William Kinderman, "Transformational Process in Beethoven's Op. 18 Quartets," in *The String Quartets of Beethoven*, ed. Kinderman, pp. 26–8.

51 Richards, *The Free Fantasia*, p. 200.

52 Ibid.

53 Kinderman, "Beethoven's Last Quartets," p. 315; see also Chapter 1, note 65.

CHAPTER 5

1 See Ensemble Oktopus, "Mark Andre riss. 2," available at https://www.youtube.com/watch?v=fKJAUyI4aww&list=RD3UtOPoTIHbo&index=2, accessed August 29, 2020.

2 Martin Zenck, 'zwischen / da-zwischen'—Kategorien einer Zwischenzeit und eines Zwischenraums: zur Musik von Mark Andre, vor allem im Ensemblestück 'riss' (2014) mit Blick und Ohr auf Beethovens op. 131," *Musik-Konzepte* No. 147, ed. Ulrich Tadday (Munich: Text und Kritik, 2016), pp. 78–81.

3 Richards, *The Free Fantasia*, p. 22.

4 See Juilliard String Quartet, "Beethoven String Quartet No. 14 in C-sharp minor, Op. 131 (1st Movement)," available at https://www.youtube.com/watch?v=zApj5uJvLZQ&list=PLUnbjrK_Qmz3-, accessed August 29, 2020.

5 See Chamber Music Society of Lincoln Center, "Beethoven: String Quartet in C-sharp minor, Op. 131," available at https://www.youtube.com/watch?v=NdD-NeMIvhIo (at 7'12"), accessed August 29, 2020.

6 Witness the large number of violin concertos in that key, including Beethoven's own.

7 See Festival Wissembourg, "The Quatuor Ebène plays Beethoven Op. 131," available at https://www.youtube.com/watch?v=-ou6tfY_tkc, accessed August 29, 2020.

8 Herre and Köhler (eds.), *Ludwig van Beethovens Konversationshefte*, 8:182 (emphasis original).

9 Ibid., 8:164.

10 Ibid., 10:32 (re. Berlin performance), 46–7, 52, 138, 164, and 167 (re. quartet players wanting to see or copy out the quartet).

11 Ibid., 10:224. See also letter from Beethoven conceived on 27 September 1826, and written on the following day by his nephew; Brandenburg (ed.), *Ludwig van Beethoven. Briefwechsel* 6, no. 2215:295, n. 1.

12 See Herre and Köhler (eds.), *Ludwig van Beethovens Konversationshefte*, vol. 10, regarding Op. 133; the premier of Op. 130 took place in March 1826.

13 Anon., "Nachrichten. Wien," *Allgemeine musikalische Zeitung* 28, no. 19 (May 10, 1826), cols. 310–11.

14 Winter, *Compositional Origins*, p. 115.

15 William Weber, "Did People Listen in the 18th Century?," *Early music* 25, no. 4 (1997), p. 689.

16 See my *Cultivating String Quartets in Beethoven's Vienna* (Woodbridge, UK: Boydell & Brewer, 2017), pp. 176–97.

17 On this subject, see Christina Bashford, "Learning to Listen: Audiences for Chamber Music in Early-Victorian London," *Journal of Victorian Culture* 4, no. 1 (1999), pp. 25–51.

18 Carl Friedrich Pohl, *Joseph Haydn*, ed. Hugo Botstiber (Leipzig: Breitkopf und Härtel, 1875–1927), 3:206. On the Pleyel scores, see Margaret Cranmer, s.v. "(1) Ignace Joseph [Ignaz Josef] Pleyel, §1: Life," in *Oxford Music Online*, available at https://www.oxfordmusiconline.com/grovemusic/grovemusic/view/10.1093/gmo/9781561592630.001.0001/omo-9781561592630-e-0000021940?rskey=lhYaLm, accessed August 29, 2020.

19 Knittel, " 'Late', Last and Least," p. 24.

20 Lenz, *Beethoven: Eine Kunststudie*, 5:261.

For the benefit of digital users, indexed terms that span two pages (e.g., 52–53) may, on occasion, appear on only one of those pages.

Figures are indicated by *f* following the page number.